THE DA [illegible] CY OF DANIEL ANDREWS

CW01628174

Assessing the Social and Economic Costs of Australia's Most Controversial Premier

Edited by Morgan Begg

Connor Court Publishing

THE DARK LEGACY OF DANIEL ANDREWS

First published in 2025 by Connor Court Publishing Pty Ltd

Po Box 7257, Redland Bay, QLD, 4165

www.connorcourtbooks.com.au

www.ipa.org.au

Copyright © the Insitute of Public Affairs 2025
All rights reserved
ISBN: 9781923568075

Cover photography: Dave Hewison Photography, www.shutterstock.com
Cover design: Lauren Scott
Printed in Australia

Contents

Contributors

Mirko Bagaric

Mirko Bagaric, Professor of Law at the Swinburne University of Technology, is an internationally renowned expert in legal rights, criminal justice, and punishment and sentencing reform. Mirko was the Dean of Law at Swinburne Law School from 2019 to 2022, and before that he was the Dean and Head of Law School at Deakin University from 2003 to 2006 and 2012 to 2015. Mirko is the author or co-author of over 30 books and 200 articles in leading Australian and international journals.

Morgan Begg

Morgan Begg, Director of Research at the Institute of Public Affairs, is an expert on rule of law and legal rights issues. Since joining the IPA in 2014, Morgan has written numerous research papers, opinion articles, essays, submissions to parliamentary inquiries, and monographs on major cultural and public policy issues. Morgan was the editor of *Peter Ridd and the Case for Academic Freedom*, published by Connor Court in 2024.

Adam Creighton

Adam Creighton, Senior Fellow and Chief Economist at the Institute of Public Affairs, is an award-winning journalist who holds a Bachelor of Economics with First Class Honours from the University of New South Wales, and a Master of Philosophy in Economics from Balliol College, Oxford. Starting his career at the Reserve Bank of Australia, Adam has written for *The Economist* and *The Wall Street Journal*, as well as *The Australian* as Economics Editor and Washington correspondent.

Gigi Foster

Gigi Foster (Professor, UNSW School of Economics; Senior Scholar, Brownstone Institute; BA Ethics, Politics and Economics, PhD Economics) is a nationally awarded university educator and was named 2019 Young Economist of the Year by the Economic Society of Australia. She co-founded Australians for Science and Freedom in 2023, is the author of dozens of academic articles and several books including *The Great Covid Panic* (2021) and *Do Lockdowns and Border Closures Serve the "Greater Good"?* (2022) and serves the community as one of Australia's leading economics communicators.

Scott Hargreaves

Scott Hargreaves is the Executive Director of the Institute of Public Affairs and Editor of the *IPA Review*. He joined the IPA staff in 2015 after more than two decades of membership, bringing with him experience across private and public organisations and state government. His career has included roles as a political adviser, consultant, corporate affairs manager, and small business operator.

Peter Jennings

Peter Jennings is the Director of Strategic Analysis Australia, the Principal of Peter Jennings Strategy Consultants Pty Ltd, and a columnist for *The Australian*. Peter was the executive director of the Australian Strategic Policy Institute (ASPI) between 2012 and 2022. He also worked in senior roles in the Australian Public Service on defence and national security. In 2025, he was lead author for the IPA publication, *No Higher Priority: A Blueprint for Immediate Action on Defence 2025-2028* and is now an IPA Adjunct Fellow.

John Lloyd

John Lloyd has held a variety of public service positions in the area of workplace relations. He was the Australian Public Service Commissioner from 2014 to 2018, and the initial Australian Building and Construction Commissioner from 2005 to 2010, with responsibility for securing lawful conduct across the Australian building and construction industry. John was also a Senior Deputy President of the Australian Industrial Relations Commission, the Red Tape Commissioner of Victoria, secretary of a state government department and various senior roles at departmental deputy secretary level. He was also a Director at the Institute of Public Affairs.

Brianna McKee

Brianna McKee is a Research Fellow and the National Manager of Generation Liberty at the Institute of Public Affairs. Brianna has contributed to publications such as *The Spectator Australia*, the *Herald Sun*, and the *Daily Telegraph*.

Kevin You

Kevin You is a Senior Fellow at the Institute of Public Affairs. His background is in the fields of political economy, industrial relations and organisational studies. Prior to joining the IPA, Kevin worked in academia – both as an educator and a researcher, as well as earning a PhD in Political Economy. His articles have been published in the *Review of Social Economy*, *Journal of Industrial Relations*, *Journal of Global Responsibility*, *Labour and Industry*, and *International Journal of Employment Studies*.

Introduction

Morgan Begg

Following the 2018 Victorian state election, Premier Daniel Andrews boasted that he led "the most progressive government" in "the most progressive state in the nation".[1] This declaration, made after one single term of Labor government, was not just a declaration of what had been, but a promise of continuing "progress".

At the conclusion of Andrews' nine years as premier, he leaves behind a state with diminished respect for personal and political freedoms, the dramatic expansion of government, and a neutered and demoralised opposition.

The calamitous state of public finances has left Victoria regarded as the Argentina of Australia[2] – a reference to the high debt Peronist mismanagement that had, until the election of Javier Milei, been overseen by a series of governments unwilling to undertake necessary reform.

The final budget update from the previous Coalition government in 2014, just ahead of that year's November election, showed net debt in the state was $21.8 billion, equivalent to 6 per cent of state economic output. By 2022-23, the final state budget handed down under Andrews' leadership, state net debt was $118 billion, or nearly 22 per cent of state economic output. Interest payments on debt alone could be equivalent to 8 per cent of state government revenue by 2028, more than double Australia's other states and territories. A federal bailout of the state's finances, that is now being openly spoken about, will put every Australian taxpayer on the hook.

But the story of Victoria is not just the fiscal and policy consequences of the Andrews era. It is the story of how the state got to this point, in which Daniel Andrews is the main character. It is clear now that Andrews was not just as an electorally successful politician; he was a tectonic figure in Victorian politics. His premiership fundamentally reshaped the state so as to enable the premier to exercise untrammelled power through a complacent media, a cowed business community, and politicised public institutions.

This book is not a biography of Daniel Andrews, but his story and personality are critical to understanding how he ruled the state.

The first thing to understand about Andrews is that, like so many other Labor politicians, he had a solely political background. Employed at an early age in an electorate office, he rose through internal party machinations to higher offices within Labor until he was preselected for the seat of Mulgrave in Melbourne's east in 2002.

Andrews joined the Labor party during the Kennett premiership and in the context of the state government undertaking significant structural reforms to reverse the fiscal collapse of the Cain-Kirner years. He came to the attention of Alan Griffin (the member for Corinella from 1993 until the seat's abolition in 1996, and then the division of Bruce in Melbourne's southeast), who was according to Sumeyya Ilanbey, journalist and Andrews' biographer:

> building a loyal socialist left sub-faction centred around Melbourne's south-east ... and he was always on the lookout for young Labor activists who might work in his electorate office and kick-start their own political careers.[3]

Andrews joined Griffin as a staffer alongside Jill Hennessy (the state member for Altona from 2010 to 2022) and Julian Hill (the federal member for Bruce since 2016) where he became involved in factional party activities:

> He was known as Griffin's 'numbers man', the main go-to-guy for the Socialist Left's branch-stacking operation in the south-eastern suburbs, a meticulous and detail-oriented young operative whom Griffin trusted wholeheartedly.[4]

At the age of 26, Andrews sought a position in the ALP head office. These positions are a result of factional battles, and Andrews emerged victorious to fill the position set aside for a member of the Socialist Left faction, against a Kim Carr backed candidate. His promotion to deputy secretary of the party, where he was responsible for campaigning, coincided not only with the successful 1999 state election, but also ALP victories in subsequent by-elections in Frankston East, Benalla (outgoing Nationals leader Pat McNamara's seat), and Burwood (Kennett's seat) through which Andrews walked away with an enhanced reputation internally. When the electoral district of Mulgrave was created ahead of the 2022 election, it was essentially set aside for Andrews.

Upon entering parliament in 2002, Andrews was immediately made a parliamentary secretary for health (outer ministry), a front bench minister in 2006, and became leader after the 2010 election. Notably, contenders for the position withdrew, believing that the party would not win in 2014. Andrews took advantage and became the man that took Labor back to the government benches.

This leads to the second thing that must be understood about Andrews. His leadership style can fairly be described as dismissive and belligerent. As one Labor insider has noted:

> An intelligent person with a lot of real skills but his problem is he genuinely thinks he's the smartest guy in the room, and he's not usually. He thinks he's the one with great political judgement, and quite often he's not. He's always more concerned with looking after his enemies than working with his friends. He holds parliament in contempt. There's a lot of support internally—you can call that loyalty—but a lot of people who support him don't really like him.

> And people don't like the way he operates with people. But he's the leader—and the thing with leaders, whether you like it or not, when you put someone in charge, you roll the dice, and the problem is until you decide to dump them, you're stuck with them. We pride ourselves on being a democracy, but we elect monarchs, and you end up having a monarchy.[5]

Victorians often witnessed the belligerence, particularly in how Andrews interacted with the media – at least on those infrequent occasions when journalists attempted to scrutinise the premier or the government. During the pandemic, Andrews would make frequent appearances before press conferences, but the response to questioning was usually batted away with references to "doing the right thing" or some spurious commitment to "follow the science". In a response to an Independent Broad-based Anti-Corruption (IBAC) report which described "evidence of misconduct and improper influence" among his senior staff, ministers, and public servants, Andrews brushed it off as an "educational report".[6] This response prompted Victorian Ombudsman Deborah Glass, whose office spent six months investigating the allegations which were the basis of the IBAC inquiry, to observe that the response "says a lot about the premier's views on corruption and integrity".[7]

One other exchange between Andrews and Paul Sakkal, a journalist at The Age, is highly illustrative. Sakkal was questioning Andrews about a statement issued by the premier in response to media reporting of a government decision to award a major contract to a union.

> Sakkal: "It's very unusual that you can't explain a statement that has your name on it, very unusual.
>
> Andrews: "Well I've issued a statement."
>
> Sakkal: "I know you've issued it, none of us understand it …Why would you issue a statement where the meaning of that statement is not clear?"
>
> Andrews: "I don't think that's what I've done, I've issued a statement, it's very clear."

A question to clarify a statement he had made was answered by reference to the statement that was being questioned.

Less well known is how Andrews operated internally to wield power within his party. The case study of how Andrews dealt with Legislative Council member and powerful state ALP figure Adem Somyurek – in which Andrews weaponised an allegation of branch-stacking to request the Socialist Left-led National Executive take over the state party, in effect giving him and his faction total control for three years – highlights how Andrews was both politically savvy and a ruthless win-at-all-costs operator.

The contradiction between Andrews' public image of a progressive who abhorred bullying and his private behaviour was well-known within the party and also in the broader bureaucracy. An inquiry by Ombudsman Glass found "a culture of fear in the upper echelons of the public service that does not support frank and fearless advice."[8]

Indeed, direct control of the government from the premier's office was a hallmark of the Andrews era. Reportedly, Andrews had 90 staffers and advisers employed in his office, compared to fewer than ten under Steve Bracks two decades earlier. On 2021 figures, a total of 286 people were employed as ministerial advisers, all of whom ultimately reported to the premier. Major decisions, regardless of portfolio, were usually made in the premier's office.

At the same time, the tentacles of Andrews extended beyond ministerial offices to the public service itself. At one time, over 1,000 were employed in the Department of Premier and Cabinet (triple what it was in 2014) which by reputation was seen as an extension of the premier's office. Labor aligned personnel were appointed to key public service positions. Former advisers to Andrews were appointed to: manage the government's $2 billion Breakthrough Victoria Fund; the Office of the Governor; departmental Secretary and Deputy Secretary level positions; the ill-fated 2026 Commonwealth Games organising committee; the Suburban Rail Loop Authority; the Major Transport Infrastructure Authority; Victoria Police; VicHealth; the North East

Rail Link Project; Rail Projects Victoria, and South East Water. In one illustrative example, one former Andrews adviser was appointed to the state Gambling and Casino Control Commission, while another former adviser found work for the gaming lobby group Responsible Wagering Australia.

This ties into the third thing to know about Andrews – the basing of decision making on short term political expediency. If the ideal of the public service was to offer fearless and frank advice to the government of the day, then overwhelming the public service with partisan appointments and running it with a "culture of fear" would make it all the easier for Andrews to implement his political agenda.

Likewise, decisions on particular policy grounds were made with seemingly no regard for long term cost or consequences. Melbourne underwent the world's longest lockdown on the basis that it would save lives today, but as **Gigi Foster** explains, the costs were far in excess of the lives saved. **Mirko Bagaric** explains how the rule of law was cast aside under the criminalisation of everyday life that took place in illogical and inconsistent ways, often where the behaviour restricted had no connection to the harm supposedly prevented.

On energy, **Kevin You** recounts how Andrews' devotion to emissions reduction targets and wind and solar plays well in the media but has severely undermined energy affordability and reliability. On education, **Brianna McKee** chronicles how schools were used to socially engineer young Victorians under the guise of nominally anti-bullying programmes, such as Safe Schools, of which Victoria was a national first-mover.

And then there's the issue of finances and public infrastructure. The dramatic expansion of public spending not only enlarged the state, but served to enrich a web of private oligopolies dependent on the public purse, particularly those involved in construction, roads, and transport. The rush to spend money on big infrastructure projects has coincided with rapid concentration in the construction industry through mergers and acquisitions. RMIT's Dr David Hayward found in 2023 that of the

33 listed public private partnerships in Victoria, 20 of them featured one of six construction conglomerates worth a combined value of more than $40 billion.

Adam Creighton describes how the Andrews government overturned the formerly bipartisan commitment formed in the wake of the Cain-Kirner financial collapse, to maintain the state's AAA credit rating, budget surpluses, and low levels of public debt. **John Lloyd** catalogues the payoff to unions in industrial relations changes, particularly as they relate to the construction and infrastructure sector. And **Peter Jennings** reveals how Andrews spearheaded an unprecedented foreign relations push to get China to pay for it through the 'Belt and Road Initiative', a global infrastructure investment strategy subsequently rejected by the federal government – which is actually constitutionally responsible for foreign affairs – as a tool to hand powers of economic coercion to China.

In its research and analysis, the Institute of Public Affairs has warned over several years that while Victoria had in the past been the economic and cultural centre of Australia, all critical indicators of financial management, such as debt, taxation, and public sector growth, reveal Victoria has become the worst performing state by a wide and growing margin.

The time has passed when voters could elect a new government to simply manage the problem. Victorians hopeful for future governments to be free from the turmoil of dramatic correction must be prepared for disappointment.

Following the state's financial collapse in the early 1990s, the Kennett-led Coalition embarked on a bold reform program to restore the state's finances and economic reputation. The difference then was that Kennett in opposition recognised the scale of the problem and was able to articulate a way out. As columnist and political commentator Terry Barnes notes:

> What [the 2018 and 2022 state elections] tells the opposition is

> that it needs to revisit Kennett's landslide victory in 1992. Kennett won not just because the then John Cain-Joan Kirner Government had virtually bankrupted the state. He won because he offered a comprehensive plan to deal with the mess and was frank with the electorate that there would need to be pain to attain eventual gain. In short, Kennett knew what he stood for and where he was going – not just for the next term, but for decades – and Victorian voters needed that reassurance to remove that discredited Labor government.[9]

In contrast, the current state opposition is not bold and does not clearly articulate its values. It also does not know how to win: at current numbers the Coalition party-rooms will go to the election with just six candidates who have previously experienced winning a state election. The vast majority of candidates will head into the 2026 state election with people who only know the Andrews style of government.

But it is critical that this not become the new normal. Victoria is less democratic than it was ten years ago. It is less free than it was ten years ago. It is more divided than it was ten years ago. To paraphrase Margaret Thatcher's famous aphorism, the state is demonstrating what happens when "you eventually run out of other people's money". Victoria must change course.

Things will get worse before they get better. If the near decade of Andrews was tumultuous, then another decade of tumult may be required to put things back in order. Public sector numbers will need to be cut. The corporate nexus between government and contractors will need to be broken. The sweetheart deals for unions on government projects ended. An aggressive rethink of the role of government through deregulation and the abolition of qangos and agencies performing non-essential work will be needed to induce productive enterprises to return to the state.

There will be no easy way out for Victoria but, to quote Margaret Thatcher again, "there is no alternative".

1

Point of no return? The chronic mismanagement of Victoria's finances

Adam Creighton

Even if unclear to the average voter, Daniel Andrews' most documented legacy – and quite possibly the most harmful – is perhaps in the realm of public finance. In less than a decade, the Andrews government transformed Victoria from one of the most fiscally prudent jurisdictions in the country to one of the most indebted, with painful years of adjustment ahead for Victorians and potentially the rest of Australia too.

On public finances, Andrews' nine-year premiership was characterised by a growing prioritisation of short-term political expediency, manifested mainly in reckless expenditure on infrastructure, over the long-term welfare of Victorian taxpayers.

The figures are startling. In his last budget before leaving office in late 2023, Andrews projected net debt to surge to a forecast $171 billion over the next four years – almost eight times the 2019 level.

As it turned out, that final Andrews budget was optimistic. Jacinta

Allan, his political successor and senior cabinet minister throughout the Andrews government, forecast net debt in her second budget to rise similarly dramatically from $155 billion to $194 billion.

Using a broader estimate, including government non-financial corporations, net debt is now poised to rise from $182 billion to $235 billion by mid-2029. Interest payments on the state's debt, using the same broader measure, are expected to surge 68 per cent to $11.9 billion over the forward estimates. That's on track to absorb a quarter of the state's total annual own-source taxation revenue, crowding out spending on health, transport, and justice.

While all Australian federal and state governments have borrowed and spent excessively since the Covid pandemic, Victoria's behaviour has easily been the most extravagant. Its net debt more than tripled from 2020 to 2023, compared with a 160 per cent increase in New South Wales and around 150 per cent in other mainland states.[10]

Chart 1.1: Net government debt in each state since 2003

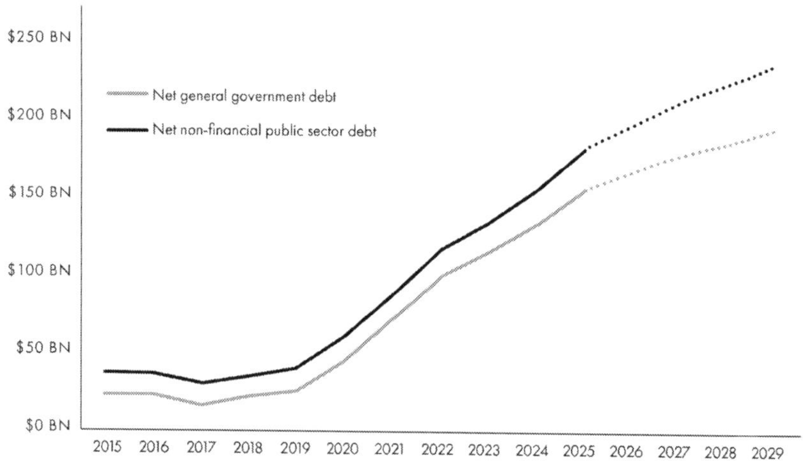

Source: Victorian Treasury documents

To put it starkly, total annual state outlays earmarked for the 2026 financial year were $107 billion, up from less than $70 billion before 2020 – a 55 per cent increase, vastly in excess of the state's population growth of around 8 per cent over the same period and similarly ahead of inflation.

Thanks to Andrews' mismanagement, Victoria no longer holds a AAA credit rating from any major agency – a significant symbolic and financial blow that underscores the state's deteriorating credibility. Both S&P Global and Moody's downgraded the state in 2020 and 2021, citing ballooning debt, persistent operating deficits, and rising interest burdens. At AA, Victoria is now the lowest-rated mainland state in Australia.[11]

Chart 1.2 Net state government debt as a percentage of gross state product

Source: IPA

The deterioration didn't begin with Covid, which the government's apologists often cite as an excuse, but it didn't begin on day one of the Andrews premiership either. Indeed, Andrews began his lengthy term evincing broadly the same degree of fiscal prudence his immediate Labor predecessors demonstrated. When his veteran Treasurer Tim Pallas handed down his first budget in May 2015, the state's net debt stood at $21.5 billion, a level already twice that of NSW, a significantly more populous state, suggesting a need for prudence. Three years later, in June 2018, Victoria's net debt had actually declined to under $20 billion.

But the government's behaviour changed radically after winning a second term, when the May 2019 budget – still pre-pandemic – projected general government net debt would more than double to $55 billion by mid-2023. That proved to be a gross underestimate and a taste of things to come, although it didn't hurt Labor's re-election chances; it would storm back into government for a third term in late 2022. By the time of the delayed 2020 pandemic budget – released in November that year – the government had pencilled in a tripling of net debt from $44 billion to $154 billion over the next four years.

That surge was not solely driven by the costs of so-called public health measures. Indeed, total state government spending on Covid related measures, over the three financial years to June 2022, was $35.8 billion, according to a fiscal retrospective published by the Treasury in 2024.[12] That's well under half of Andrews' debt legacy.

In June 2023, a few months before he retired from politics, Victoria's net debt stood at almost $117 billion, a $96 billion absolute increase, or more than five times greater than what he had inherited from the Napthine government in November 2014. Under Andrews' tenure, Victoria had swapped places with NSW, which in 2023 had net debt of $92 billion.

Victoria, according to S&P's analysis released in February, had operating expenses $69 billion higher over the three years to 2023 – long after Covid had passed – than had been forecast in the final pre-pandemic budget.

Lockdowns – which infamously lasted longer in Melbourne than in any other major city in the world – may have hurt revenue as they shuttered businesses for months on end. But it was government choices, not public health necessity, that underpinned the extraordinary budget blowout.

The politicisation of infrastructure, not Covid, explains the bulk of the cost blowout. Australia's population was growing rapidly everywhere, but only in Victoria did annual infrastructure investment explode from a steady $5 billion a year over the decade to 2016, to nearly $25 billion in the 2024 financial year.

Andrews launched infrastructure megaprojects on a scale never before seen in Victoria, often with little to no cost-benefit analysis. Projects were routinely announced with no federal funding secured and scant regard for how they would be paid for. The Suburban Rail Loop (SRL), which would link outer suburbs of Melbourne in a radial fashion, was emblematic. Touted as a transformational piece of infrastructure, the SRL was announced before a business case was released, and even now remains only partially funded. Internal government documents and senior Labor figures have since admitted the hope was always to pressure Canberra into paying for a third, and for land value capture to pay for another third – a strategy that appears increasingly fanciful. On her trip to China in September 2025, Premier Allan had even resorted to asking Chinese investors to help make up the shortfall.[13]

First announced in 2018 with a mooted price tag of $50 billion, some observers now expect the total cost across the three stages to surpass $200 billion. The government's predilection for projects that would help it politically was already clear in 2015, when Andrews cancelled the East-West freeway link at a cost of more than $1 billion, to mollify Greens voters in inner northern metropolitan seats who were implacably opposed.[14]

One senior Labor figure confided, on the condition of anonymity, that they didn't believe the government was ever serious about building the SRL when it was announced, seeing it instead as a clever political ruse to win votes in marginal seats that would ultimately be walked back. Other projects, such as electrifying the rail lines to Melton and Werribee, bringing them into the suburban network and taking pressure off regional services, would have cost less and brought greater benefits. Almost incredibly in hindsight, Andrews quashed a proposal from a consortium of investors including even Labor aligned IFM Investors to build a high-speed rail link from the airport to the city, which would have cost Victorian taxpayers $5 billion and could at least be justified on the basis that Melbourne is one of the few major cities in the world without a train connecting its airport to its CBD.[15]

The North East Link was another example. Initially budgeted at $10 billion, it is now expected to cost $26 billion. The West Gate Tunnel has nearly doubled in cost due to mismanagement and environmental remediation issues. Other examples include the level crossing removal program, originally forecast to cost $5 billion, which has now exceeded $10 billion, and the decision to massively expand the size of the National Gallery of Victoria. Even the Frankston Hospital upgrade is on track to cost over $1.1 billion, more than double the forecast in 2019.

The excessive and growing influence of the CFMEU, the most powerful construction union in the state, has been a major factor in rising construction costs across Australia, up around 30 per cent in recent years.[16] The militant union, long accused of criminal activities, has used aggressive industrial tactics and restrictive work practices to increase its influence over the more politically moderate Australian Workers Union, which once competed to oversee the workforces of state government projects, helping keep a cap on costs. Even unionised traffic controllers on major sites have reportedly been paid over $200,000 a year – more than double what police or nurses might earn. Far from confront it, Andrews appeared to ensure the CFMEU would oversee every single major construction project in the state. Even the ABC's state political reporter Richard Willingham wrote in 2024 that in Victoria "the CFMEU is at its strongest and the Andrews-Allan government has always kept it on side."[17] The major builders know that dealing with the union is now just part of doing business.

Then there was the 2026 Commonwealth Games. Marketed as a decentralised triumph for regional development, the Games became a textbook example of fiscal incompetence when it was cancelled barely more than a year after it was announced. Initial cost estimates of

$2.6 billion ballooned to a claimed $6.9 billion, though the Auditor-General later questioned the credibility of that figure. The cancellation cost $589 million, including $380 million in compensation payments, without a single race run. Cynics noted the Games, which would have helped the government win votes in marginal regional seats where many of the events were to be staged, were announced in early 2022 before the state election. Their cancellation barely more than a year later created an impression that a government floundering in debt might not have intended to host them at all.

Beyond infrastructure, Andrews presided over a bloated political machine. The premier's private office had 86 staff in 2022, dwarfing the 51 employed by Prime Minister Scott Morrison at the time. Such overreach was emblematic of a broader approach to government that increasingly blurred the line between public administration and political campaigning. Over the eight years to 2022 around 20 per cent of new jobs in Victoria were in the public sector, a share that has exploded to 70 per cent of new jobs since then, according to IPA research from late 2024.[18]

The Victorian public sector workforce grew from 277,670 in June 2015, including 37,942 in the core public service, to 382,823, including 57,345 in the public service, in June 2024. That's growth of 38 per cent overall and a remarkable 51 per cent for the bureaucracy. Almost one-in-ten workers in Victoria now work directly for the state. This combined with the extensive infrastructure projects commissioned by the government but delivered by the private sector, means a significant portion of economic activity and employment is now dependent on the largesse of government to survive. That this creates a powerful and intractable barrier to reform cannot be understated and in turn has formed a powerful bulwark for Labor's electoral fortunes.

Where previous Labor governments such as those led by Steve Bracks and John Brumby had carefully cultivated a fiscally conservative image – even enshrining a commitment to a recurrent surplus – the Andrews government did the opposite.

Chart 1.3 Net Victorian general government debt since 1990

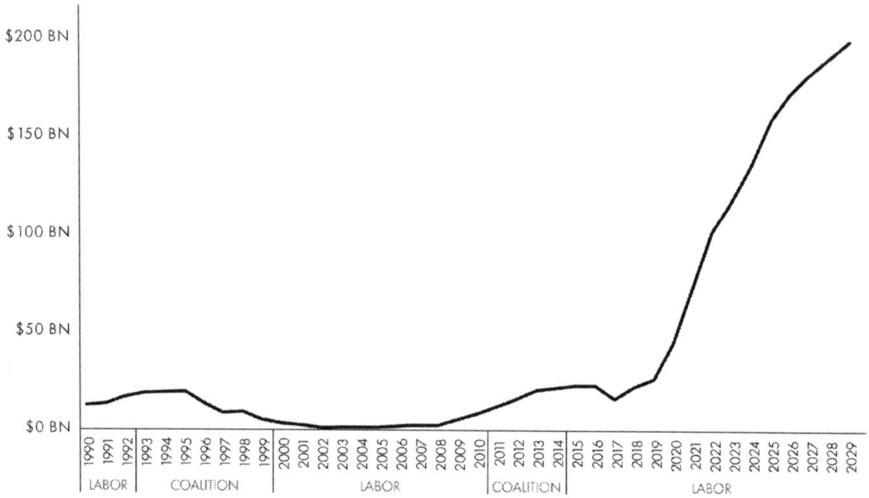

Source, IPA: Victorian Treasury documents

Indeed, the contrast with the Bracks and Brumby governments, in power from 1999 to 2010, is instructive. They were fiscal moderates who had inherited the political scars of the Cain-Kirner economic collapse in the early 1990s. Brumby, as treasurer and later premier, delivered major infrastructure such as EastLink on time and under budget, often claiming publicly it remains the cheapest toll road ever built in Australia. These leaders were guided by the view that Labor must prove itself as a responsible economic manager to earn the right to govern.

One of the more common lines of defence used by the Andrews government and its supporters is that debt servicing costs remain lower than under Joan Kirner's Labor government in the early 1990s. Back then, interest payments absorbed around 15 per cent of budget outlays because the level of interest rates was so much higher. Today the equivalent figure is around 7 per cent. But this is false assurance, given greater levels of global uncertainty that could see a sharp surge in interest rates, which would apply to a much larger sum of outstanding debt in nominal terms.

Another favoured deflection comes from comparisons to the 1960s, when net debt reportedly reached 57 per cent of Gross State Product under Liberal Premier Sir Henry Bolte. But Bolte's debt was mostly held by revenue-generating state-owned enterprises such as the Gas and Fuel Corporation, which have long since been privatised.

Andrews' debt, by contrast, is predominantly held by the general government sector, with far fewer revenue-producing assets to service it. And whereas Bolte's liabilities were associated with infrastructure that generated long-term productivity gains, much of Andrews' spending was directed toward vanity projects and the ongoing expansion of the public service, which even veteran Labor figures have privately expressed concern about.

Soaring debt was hardly a function of restraint in taxation, which soared during the Andrews administration. According to one analysis, the Andrews government introduced 63 new and increased taxes, fees, and charges. Among these were the Covid Debt Levy, first pitched as temporary, but which has become permanent, raising over $1.1 billion a year from over-taxed businesses in 2025. Land tax thresholds were lowered to as low as $50,000 (from a previous threshold of $300,000) and rates increased dramatically, hitting small investors and retirees. A new mental health levy extracts another $1.1 billion a year from employers in added payroll tax. Registration fees, such as for births, deaths, and marriages, were hiked. Despite these revenue increases, Victoria continues to run large operating deficits.

Victorian taxpayers are now the most burdened in the nation. Total tax revenue is projected to rise by over 22 per cent by 2029, yet the budget remains structurally in deficit. Even massive revenue windfalls during the Covid recovery period – when property markets and payrolls surged – were spent rather than saved.

The question now is whether Victoria can unwind the debt trap it has built for itself. That will require a level of political courage not yet visible from the Allan government, which has shown little appetite for reform. Allan's May 2025 budget was a continuation of Andrews' legacy: optimistic assumptions, vague references to future savings, and an almost religious commitment to infrastructure spending, not to mention a contempt for private business epitomised by her August 2025 call to mandate two days a week working from home.

Reform would require major cuts to a bloated public service, program cuts, and significant reductions in taxation, especially on investors and small business.

The assumption has long been that economic growth will lift the state out of its fiscal hole. But there is little evidence to support that. Victoria's productivity growth has stalled. Population growth has slowed relative to New South Wales and Queensland. And interest rates, while lower than in the 1990s, are no longer near zero. Debt servicing costs are already approaching $12 billion a year. That number could rise rapidly if borrowing costs increase even modestly.

The Allan government is paying over $2 million to consultants at Ad Astra Corporate Advisory to identify potential asset sales. But the cupboard is nearly bare. The government has already sold the Land Titles Office, leased the Port of Melbourne, and privatised VicRoads licensing and registration. What remains is politically toxic or legally complex to divest.

On paper the state has well over $420 billion in long-term assets, but much of this, such as Crown land, can't realistically be sold. Public backlash would be fierce. Fire sales would likely depress prices. And as Kennett-era veterans will recall, large-scale privatisation only works when you act quickly and decisively at the beginning of a term of office.

The government also appointed Helen Silver, former head of the Department of Premier and Cabinet, to identify $3.3 billion in savings. But the effort appears half-hearted. No serious cuts to the public service have been proposed. No major programs have been wound back. And the looming 2026 state election makes any politically costly move unlikely.

Even if the Allan government wanted to act, it may now be too late. To achieve meaningful savings through public service reform requires both time and political capital. Kennett made deep cuts, imposed a new poll tax, and signalled major asset sales within months of taking office. The longer a government delays, the harder those decisions become.

Some defenders of the government point to the similar behaviour and challenges of all Australian states, which together enjoyed $146 billion more in revenue over the four years to 2023 than had been forecast before the pandemic, yet spent $212 billion more. Queensland's net debt is forecast to triple. South Australia and Western Australia also face rising borrowing costs. But none have gone as far, as fast, or as carelessly as Victoria.

Australia's High Court has undoubtedly left the states in a difficult fiscal position. The pervasive centralisation of taxation powers has left the states financially dependent on Commonwealth grants. Despite the lack of genuine fiscal independence, Andrews nonetheless made the decisions to embark on the most ambitious infrastructure agenda in the nation, inflate the size of the public sector, and maintain pandemic era public spending levels into 2025 and beyond – and there is now a very real prospect that the Commonwealth will ultimately be required to step in and bail out the state.

Daniel Andrews may have governed with extraordinary political skill. But his fiscal legacy is one of recklessness, overreach, and denial – which more and more Victorians are beginning to realise amid reports the former premier often faces abuse when he ventures out of his home. He leaves behind a state in financial peril, with few levers left to pull.

In his eulogy for former Labor premier John Cain, who died in 2019, Andrews recalled being told by his political mentor and hero "never to waste a day". He certainly didn't – but he's left a legacy of waste and mismanagement that could take a decade or more to reverse.

2

Liberties lost: The assault on Victoria's freedoms

Morgan Begg

Prior to 2020 it was rare to see the word "lockdown" used by anyone other than a prison warden in the context of managing inmates. This makes sense because it is a fundamentally totalitarian response requiring the rights and liberties of a free people to be summarily discarded. However, in response to the Covid-19 pandemic, Victoria itself became the prison, and the Andrews government the warden casting aside the rights and liberties of what we thought were a free people.

But were Victorians truly a free people? An appraisal of the years preceding the first Covid lockdowns reveals a persistent degrading of Victoria's liberal traditions through legislative reforms and heated invective against the premier's political and ideological enemies that softened up the state for the imposition of Covid overreach. Indeed, the Andrews government was visibly hostile to traditional freedoms of speech, association, and religion, with the attacks on these rights routinely justified on the basis of saving and protecting people in the community – a refrain that became a hallmark of Andrews' Covid-era rhetoric.

A recurring theme throughout the first half of the Andrews premiership was the use of health-based arguments, relying on the good-natured concern of Victorians for the wellbeing of other Victorians, to make incursions into individual liberties. This is what conservative commentator Rod Dreher refers to as "therapeutic totalitarianism", where people are manipulated to cede without complaint their rights on the basis that it will help the community (as distinct from other forms of soft totalitarianism, such as 'iron fist in velvet glove', which refers to restrictions being imposed to save people from themselves).

To be clear, several Australian jurisdictions enforced harsh public health rules, but no other state or territory was close to imposing the same level of irrational and arbitrary rules as Victoria. Research by the Institute of Public Affairs in April 2020 revealed how Victoria was the only state to impose bans on outdoor recreational activities such as fishing or playing golf, driving in their car, or even sitting on a park bench.[19] Researchers from the Australian National University, the University of New South Wales, and Oxford University assessed Covid policy responses as part of a worldwide stringency index, finding that Victoria imposed the most consistently stringent policies during 2021,[20] which is also the period in which Melbourne surpassed Buenos Aires' record for the most days under lockdown.[21]

Throughout six separate lockdowns totalling 262 days between March 2020 and October 2021, Victorians were required to comply with a variety of restrictions on everyday human activity, including a requirement to remain in their place of residence for 23 hours of the day with an allowance to leave for only four narrowly specified reasons. For the first time in Australia's history a curfew was introduced which forced Victorians to stay in their homes between 8pm and 5am. Victorians could not gather in groups of more than five and could only do so outside. A travel restriction of 5km from one's home was introduced and the sinister sounding 'Ring of Steel' divided Victoria in two, separating metropolitan Melbourne from regional Victoria. Other normalities of human life were upended; there was no school attendance for the better part of two years, no church attendance allowed, direct human interaction impeded by social distancing rules, and even basic communication impeded by way of the mandatory introduction of masks in all public spaces, and indeed many private ones.

In trying to explain the curfews, Andrews declared that their introduction "is not about human rights. It is about human life". This attitude revealed the vision of life held by the government – being merely to not be dead. This contrasts with the Western tradition that acknowledges that the value of life is integrally bound up in in the preservation of human dignity, of which natural rights are a central feature.

The origins of Andrews' lockdown laws

The decisions made by the Victorian government to impose Covid rules were ostensibly pursuant to legislation conferring power on the state's chief health officer (a political appointment of the state government). This legislation, the *Public Health and Wellbeing Act 2008*, is not "normal" public health legislation. While Victoria has long made provision for authorities to deal specifically with persons infected by contagious diseases and to disinfect properties, laws did not empower the state to detain uninfected people or create statewide emergency areas before Daniel Andrews, as health minister in the late-2000s, overhauled the state's public health legislation that enabled the government to impose lockdowns. The powers included:

- Detain any person or group of persons in the emergency area for the period reasonably necessary to eliminate or reduce a serious risk for public health;
- Restrict the movement of any person or group of persons within the emergency area;
- Prevent any person or group of persons from entering the emergency area;
- Give any other direction that the authorised officer considers is reasonably necessary to protect public health.[22]

Prior to the *Public Health and Wellbeing Act 2008* coming into force in 2010, the pre-existing *Health Act 1958* was limited to empowering the state to prescribe an emergency area and to prevent people from entering or leaving the prescribed area. This distinction is critical: a government that wanted to control the movement of people under the pre-Andrews laws would need to carefully designate an area that people were stopped from entering or leaving. A government that wanted to control the movement of people under the Andrews laws could merely declare the entire state an emergency area and thereby control any movement of any person within that prescribed area.[23] And that is exactly what occurred in Victoria under the first of many declarations of a state of emergency on 16 March 2020.

Moreover, the pre-Andrews public health laws were notable for the preservation of democratic oversight of the emergency proclamation process. Subsections 123(3)(b) and 123(4) of the *Health Act 1958* prior to its repeal provided that a proclamation may be revoked by a resolution of either house of the state parliament. Moreover, if the parliament was not sitting at the time the emergency was proclaimed, a petition of 20 members of the Legislative Assembly or 30 members of the whole parliament requesting parliament be summoned would ensure the parliament must meet as soon as possible. Not only were such democratic controls discarded in the Andrews laws, parliament itself was entirely sidelined during the pandemic. This ranged from the periodic cancellation of sitting days, to the constitutionally dubious act of attempting to exclude MPs from attending parliament who did not prove they were vaccinated against Covid – a contempt of parliament that seemingly contradicted those provisions of the state constitution that preserve the rights and privileges of members of parliament to exercise their duties without obstruction.[24]

The Andrews public health laws that came into force in 2010 were fully weaponised ten years later. But while this explains the legal background to the imposition of lockdowns, there was a sustained period of the Andrews premiership from 2014 to 2020 in which Victorians became accustomed to government winding back traditional freedoms.

Daniel Andrews and "therapeutic totalitarianism"

The therapeutic totalitarianism approach relies on shaming people who object to proposed laws for wanting to harm others. An early example from the Andrews government were amendments made in 2015 to the *Public Health and Wellbeing Act 2008* that gave the government the power to make regulations which criminalise any type of behaviour within 150 metres of premises at which abortions are provided. The criticisms that this was obviously excessive were drowned out by claims that the laws were necessary so that women would be able to "access lawful medical services free from harassment and intimidation".[25] Public harassment and intimidation is already an offence, but this rhetoric disguised the purpose of the law, which was to criminalise benign activities: the first person arrested under the legislation breached the laws by attempting to hand a pamphlet to a couple entering a clinic in East Melbourne.[26]

Andrews extended this rhetorical tactic by medicalising non-health issues to stifle dissent, ensuring opponents of government policy could be accused of causing harm by "denying the science" put forward by "experts". This was evident in the premier's vehement subordination of open debate to straw man arguments and *ad hominem* attacks. In a media release regarding the legislation of Safe Schools, a highly controversial curriculum package which normalised radical gender theories under the guise of harm reduction, Andrews referred opponents as "dinosaurs"[27] and "bigots" [who] ought to be ashamed of themselves in terms of their views".[28] When then Prime Minister Malcolm Turnbull opened the floor to a public debate on same-sex marriage by way of plebiscite, Andrews accused Turnbull of imposing "one last hurdle, one last insult" that will "hurt people" and attempted to "concern troll" the prime minister by suggesting it would tarnish his reputation.[29]

This rhetoric became a hallmark of Andrews' attacks on Christians in public life. In speaking of Australian tennis legend Margaret Court, he not only diminished her tremendous talents and success, but refused to acknowledge any validity in her religious views when he stated that

"Grand Slam wins don't give you some right to spew hatred and create division … I don't want to give this person's disgraceful, bigoted views any oxygen."[30]

Figure 2.1: An example of the divisive social media post from Andrews

When Andrew Thorburn was appointed the CEO of the Essendon Football Club in October 2022, Andrews led a concerted public campaign to reverse the appointment on the basis that Thorburn was associated with a church that espoused religious views that the premier disagreed with. Andrews said the views he was ascribing to Thorburn were "absolutely appalling … that kind of intolerance, that kind of hatred, bigotry. It is just wrong."[31] In particular, Andrews leaned into the therapeutic argument, asserting that due to the views the premier thought Thorburn held, "people are harming themselves and, sometimes, taking their own lives because of bigotry and prejudice".[32] A day into the public cancel campaign, Thorburn resigned was maligned in a club statement on his way out..[33] In this way, Andrews was able to achieve the removal of Christians from the public sphere by increasing the cost of speaking out or acting in accordance with their conscience, without passing laws or wielding power directly.

Probably most famous was the premier's treatment of Cardinal George Pell over unproven – if not disproven – allegations of child abuse. In 2020 the High Court of Australia unanimously overturned a Victorian court's 2018 conviction of Cardinal Pell, due to the jury's failure at trial to properly assess all the evidence and entertain a reasonable doubt that the offending had taken place. Key to the flaws in the prosecution of Pell was the *Jury Directions Act 2015* passed by the Andrews government, which includes in section 39 a rule that a trial judge "must not say, or suggest in any way, to the jury that ... the victim's evidence should be scrutinised with great care". In other words, the testimony of accusers is to be in effect assumed to be valid, an inexcusable violation of the presumption of innocence, one of the most basic legal rights we enjoy in English law. Following the High Court's decision overturning the Victorian court, Andrews contemptuously said:

> I make no comment about today's High Court decision. But I have a message for every single victim and survivor of child sex abuse. I see you. I hear you. I *believe* you.[34] [Emphasis added]

It is difficult to escape the conclusion that the flawed and politicised pursuit of Pell was justified because Pell – and the Church itself – represents commitments to conservative social values and culture that offends the secularism of Andrews and the Victorian political class. An institution like a church – whether Catholic or otherwise – can influence the hearts and minds of millions of people, therefore it represents a power centre that rivals the power the political class would prefer to wield itself. One cannot know if this was underlying Daniel Andrews' rhetoric against Christian figures, but what is notable is the extent of legislation passed by the Andrews government aimed at undermining religious freedoms. In the *Spectator Australia* in February 2021, I observed that the Andrews government was "the most hostile state or federal government to people of faith in Australian history".[35] This opinion was reinforced later by *The Australian* columnist Greg

Sheridan, who said all Victorians were being targeted by the "most dedicated and consistent anti-Christian government in Australian history".[36]

In addition to the abortion access zone laws, that made it an offence to engage in any kind of communication, such as silent prayer, in a prohibited area, the government also attacked prayer through the passage of the *Change or Suppression (Conversion) Practices Prohibition Act 2021*. The laws created criminal penalties and gave new powers to the state human rights commission to outlaw "carrying out a religious practice, including but not limited to, a prayer-based practice" in relation to a person's internal conflict about their sexual orientation or gender identity.[37] When the legislation was passed, Andrews released a disingenuous media statement commenting on those that opposed the law and stating that "bigotry doesn't give anyone the right to tell others they are broken".[38]

In 2016, the Victorian government first proposed to amend the state's *Equal Opportunity Act 2010* to include an "inherent requirements" test for faith-based schools. The test would limit the autonomy of faith-based schools, allowing them to only impose religious requirements on staff in relation to jobs for which religious compliance was deemed inherently necessary. This is arbitrary because it misunderstands the critical importance of staff in preserving the common ethos of a faith-based school as part of the wider religious community parents seek to be involved in, making it not just an attack on faith-based schools but on mainstream families seeking to join a community of faith. The 2016 amendments were defeated in the Legislative Council then, but the government retained its commitment to make these changes, passing such laws in 2021.[39]

Another major pre-Covid reform was the introduction of mandatory reporting laws in 2019. These laws compel clergy to violate the seal of confession if a priest has a "reasonable belief" of actual or likely physical or sexual child abuse, by reporting this to child protection authorities. The practical flaws with this are obvious: how can the government prove that a confession took place if it is a private ritual? How can a priest report a person if the confession is made confidentially? And if confessions about child abuse are so common – they likely aren't – wouldn't requiring confessions to be forwarded to the authorities simply put an end to confessions? And perhaps most importantly of all, did the government even contemplate that a priest would opt for prison over breaking the seal of confession, one of the seven sacraments and an act of worship between the penitent and God? A cynic might observe that given the obvious unenforceability of the rule, the reforms were intended to distract from child protection failures by suggesting the real problem was with ministers of religion.

The government did not only target Christians. In 2019, the state government began the process of reforming the state's anti-vilification laws by expanding the number of "protected attributes" to include not only race and religion but also sex, gender, disability and sexual orientation (and more), and to make it unlawful for a person to engage in conduct that "a reasonable person would consider hateful".[40] This is a threshold that rejects even the façade of an objective legal standard or predictable definition that would give people confidence in how it could be applied consistently. It is a proposal so broad that it would bring potentially any opinion about any contentious matter within the scope of unlawfulness.

These actions were a sure indication that Victoria under Andrews did not prioritise basic freedoms and legal rights. These are precarious at the best of times, but when the state was tested by pandemic, the Victorian government went down the easy path. This was despite the prevalence of public health plans that sought to balance public health priorities with proportionality, respect for individual rights, responsibilities, and freedom, and the minimisation of social disruption in the knowledge that "the risk is not the same across population groups".[41]

The inevitability of the Zoe Buhler case

The image of a pregnant Ballarat woman, dressed in her pyjamas, being rounded up in her own kitchen by black clad Victoria Police officers, perfectly encapsulated Victoria's slide into a police state. The woman, Zoe Buhler, was a 28-year-old mother who had posted on Facebook about a forthcoming protest against the government's public health regulations.

At the time of the arrest in September 2020, Ballarat was under similar restrictions to more populous Melbourne, despite only having a handful of active cases at the time. In the post about the anti-lockdown gathering, Buhler stressed that "all social-distancing measures are to be followed so we don't get arrested please. Please wear a mask unless you have a medical reason not to." But arrested she was. This was not the application of the law, but the brutal abuse of it.

The police claimed that Buhler's Facebook post, in relation to a public gathering, incited others to breach public health orders restricting the number of people that could gather in public at any one time. Because of this, Buhler was arrested by Victoria Police and charged under section 321G of the *Crimes Act 1958* (Vic), which makes it an offence to "incite a person to pursue a course of conduct which will involve the commission of an offence".

There were two key flaws with this: the first is that the police were making an arrest without a warrant, but in order to do this the police need to reasonably believe that a person has committed an indictable offence. Yet, Victoria Police never established a *prima facie* case that the offence of incitement had ever taken place. The offence of incitement requires an inciting act and that another person was incited to commit an offence. However, in arresting Buhler, the police were acting on the assumption that inciting acts could be made to the public at large and that someone, somewhere, at some time, might have been invited to commit an offence. This kind of interpretation gives police immense scope to criminalise speech.

The second key issue was whether the government had actually ever made protests a crime. The offence of incitement requires a person to be incited to commit an offence, but the police were acting on the assumption that the public health orders amounted to criminal laws. The enabling legislation in the *Public Health and Wellbeing Act 2008* empowering public officials to make public health order was ambiguous on this question. Laws that prevent or punish public harms, rather than direct or personal harms, are usually administrative in nature and only incur civil penalties, rather than criminal penalties. A compelling reason for this is that a bureaucrat acting alone to create rules should not have the power to create new *crimes*, especially when this can have consequences that last long after the emergency period has expired, in the form of a permanent entry in a person's criminal record.

It was also wrong of the government to criminalise everyday behaviour. The classic common law rule is that "the absolute divorce of law from morality would be of fatal consequence",[42] meaning it is a mistake to criminalise conduct which is not morally flawed, such as opposing government overreach or expressing an opinion on social media.

A fair application of the law ought to find that there was no legal basis for Victoria Police arresting Buhler. But this was a question that was never answered definitively: in September 2022 – two full years after the original arrest – when Buhler's case was about to be heard in the courts, the crown denied Buhler's day in court and withdrew the charges.

Buhler did not get her answers, but her arrest did achieve something: it showed for all the world to see that Victoria's pandemic response was arbitrary and completely ignored principles of proportionality and the rule of law. What happened to Buhler was not a mistake or an unintended side effect, but the inevitable consequence of empowering the police to enforce, with the full force of the criminal law, the unprecedented idea that an official could declare activities "non-essential".

Rather than be embarrassed by the infamous Buhler episode, the Andrews government almost appeared to be emboldened. It passed even more laws granting itself even more draconian powers. In particular, the *Public Health and Wellbeing (Pandemic Management) Act 2021* represented a transferral of power to the executive government that was unprecedented in Australia's peacetime history. It added specific "pandemic management" powers to the *Public Health and Wellbeing Act* to enable the premier to make pandemic declarations and enable the health minister and government officials to exercise extraordinary powers during pandemic declarations. These included the power to impose indefinite lockdowns (even if there were no cases of the virus in the country), imprison people without trial, and arrest people because of their religion, political beliefs, or ethnic background, all in the absence of control or scrutiny by the parliament or the courts.[43] And the premier and health minister could rule by decree indefinitely. The powers to detain were so extraordinary that I observed in a report published in 2022 that, in casting aside the common law right of right of *habeas corpus* (that itself dates back to the *Assize of Clarendon* in 1166AD) a person detained under the laws would have fewer rights than an accused terrorist.[44]

Throughout the Andrews premiership, opposition to Andrews from the major centres of power in Victorian society – not just the political opposition, but the media, the churches and big business – failed to respond in a meaningful way to the threats posed to our way of life. Andrews changed the culture of Victoria through his style of leadership, and the legislative reforms he spearheaded had the result of minimising the place of basic freedoms, such as freedom of speech and religious liberty, and removing these from political discourse. This is a recipe for poor government, to put it mildly. Future political leaders need to recognise that Daniel Andrews leaving office, or the ALP government being beaten at the ballot box, will not remove Andrews' continuing influence over the state: only a new state political culture framed around Australia's liberal traditions can move us away from Daniel Andrews' illiberal legacy.

3

Trashing the rule of law – with impunity: The erosion of criminal justice in Victoria

Mirko Bagaric

Fundamental rule of law and jurisprudential principles that lawyers assumed were a bulwark of democracy were repeatedly trashed by the Andrews government. Under sweeping reforms instigated by Daniel Andrews, everyday conduct was criminalised, which in its most dramatic period – the pandemic period – allowed the government to hold authoritarian rule over the state.

Superfluous laws and disproportionate penalties gave the state the power to dictate the everyday lives of Victorians, from who a person was allowed to spend time with under anti-association laws to how many female fertile dogs a person could own. The most extreme example of Andrews' overextension of power was the Victorian government's response to the Covid-19 pandemic and the repressive measures implemented along with it. Victorians were harassed by police for walking outdoors on the basis of laws that were often promulgated while they were literally sleeping, and in circumstances where the behaviour had no connection to the harm sought to be prevented.

The Andrews government's abuse of the criminal law

Criminal offences traditionally deal with the most harmful and immoral forms of conduct, such as rape, assault, and robbery, and can result in citizens being subjected to public opprobrium and the most oppressive sanctions available in our legal system, including a deprivation of liberty.

From the earliest days of the Andrews premiership there was wide and unprecedented use of the criminal law as a regulatory instrument to address matters or activities that the government disagreed with.

In 2015, the Andrews government enacted severe anti-association laws that gave police the power to issue anti-association notices to any person 18 years old or older, telling them who they could not associate with.[45] In 2017, new criminal laws were introduced to regulate the breeding of cats and dogs (either for fun or for profit),[46] as well as new laws imposing criminal penalties on venues which failed to enforce prohibitions on smoking in outdoor dining areas.[47] Daniel Andrews, as premier, even boasted that the state had the most strict electoral laws in the country,[48] after it passed laws in 2018 to effectively cap democratic participation and restrict political donations to a maximum of $4,000 every four years,[49] with non-compliance resulting in fines of up to 300 penalty units (currently approximately $59,000) or two years in jail, or both.[50]

These actions formed a precursor to the Andrews government's most authoritarian abuse of the criminal law: the declared state of emergency and public health rules imposed in response to the Covid-19 pandemic.

Governments throughout Australia implemented severe restrictions during the pandemic (March 2020 to late 2021) in an attempt to limit the spread of Covid-19. The nature of the restrictions varied throughout Australia, with Victoria being subject to the longest lockdown and strictest enforcement regime. The restrictions in Melbourne were so severe that the city has taken on the dubious title of the most locked-down city in the world.[51] This resulted in part from Victoria moving to a Covid elimination strategy, and away from the "flattening the curve" strategy which had been adopted at the start of the pandemic.

The restrictions that were imposed in Victoria impacted every citizen, and in a profound manner. They involved the curtailment or negation of a number of fundamental rights, including the freedom of movement and expression, and the rights to work, education and to participate in family relations.[52] People were effectively required to stay at home unless they had a designated reason for leaving home: namely shopping for essentials; authorised work; exercise (for a limited time); caregiving or medical reasons.

It was clear from the start of the pandemic that Covid threatened the health and safety of some members of the community and hence a governmental response was necessary. In particular, it was important to ensure that people were as physically apart as could be reasonably achieved. There were a range of options that were available to governments to achieve this outcome.

The conventional manner in which governments deal with health issues is to implement a public education campaign, as occurs with regard to alcohol, tobacco, and obesity. This is a non-coercive (soft power) approach which requires governments to inform, educate, and persuade people. It was in the self-interest of people to avoid contracting Covid, and the pandemic was receiving saturated media attention at the time. Hence, it would not have been difficult to influence people to change their behaviour.

It was highlighted that the *Charter of Human Rights and Responsibilities Act 2006* (Vic), which sets out a number of fundamental rights (including the right to life and liberty), is not enforceable but rather, seeks to shape the manner in which law is interpreted and to educate the community regarding the importance of human rights. Instead of adopting an educational, soft power approach to pandemic restrictions, the Victorian government utilised the most coercive process in our system of law to shape community behaviour in response to the pandemic.

The Victorian government invoked the criminal law as the principal means through which the Covid restrictions were implemented and enforced from the commencement of the pandemic. This involved the creation of a large number of new offences, criminal sanctions, and enforcement mechanisms. Most breaches of the pandemic restrictions were criminal offences, and the most common manner in which sanctions were imposed was by infringements notices for breaches of the Chief Health Officer's Directions under section 200 of the *Public Health and Wellbeing Act 2008* (Vic).

Disturbingly, there was no parliamentary oversight of these laws. The offences and sanctions were created at the whim of the Chief Health Officer and hence circumvented the requirement for Victorian legislation to be screened for compatibility with the rights and freedoms enshrined in the *Charter of Human Rights and Responsibilities Act 2006* (Vic), such as 'freedom of movement',[53] 'freedom of expression'[54] and protection of the family.[55] Thus, it is not surprising that:

> Regrettably, human rights considerations have hardly surfaced in the political and public discourse about the usefulness and utility of employing criminal offences to combat COVID-19 in Australia.[56]

The number of new criminal laws which were created and the speed with which they were implemented during the pandemic is unprecedented in Australia. Certainly, it is not uncommon for governments to use the criminal law as a means to regulate human behaviour.[57] However, there are several important features relating to the pandemic control measures which are novel and violate a number of rule of law virtues, including the need for laws to be knowable and fair.

Criminalising everyday behaviour which often has no connection with the harm sought to be prevented demonstrates that pragmatically there does not need to be any link between the criminal law and immoral or harmful behaviour. Victoria's criminalisation of pandemic restrictions, political expression and everyday freedoms showed that the criminal law can effectively be used to suppress any conduct which the government regards as undesirable. Moreover, the government can do this without any negative consequences: political opposition to, and media scrutiny of, the government's pandemic laws throughout the period were minimal.

The reality is that there is a huge gulf between theoretical jurisprudential principles and the protections that people actually enjoy. This gap can only be closed if the public is better informed about the nature of the appropriate legal and social safeguards and are prepared to hold governments accountable for a breach of these norms. This is not the current situation in the State of Victoria.

The breadth and severity of the pandemic laws

The most defining aspect of the pandemic criminal laws was the almost blanket impact that they had on most parts of everyday life. The restrictions touched on nearly every aspect of human behaviour and relationships, from limiting the amount of time people could spend outside their front gate (at one point to one hour per day); the time of day they could leave their house (an 8pm curfew was imposed) and locations they could visit (a total prohibition was imposed on visiting other households). Children were prevented from visiting frail parents. The effect of this was that nearly every human action, no matter how innocuous (from entering a playground to filling up petrol after 8pm), was viewed through the lens of the criminal law.

Millions of people who had meticulously observed the criminal law all their lives were suddenly under the active purview of police for engaging in what was previously routine and harmless conduct. This was graphically highlighted by footage of police sometimes questioning elderly citizens sitting on park benches—an activity that was prohibited as part of the lockdown. Opposition to the restrictions resulted in some relatively small-scale protests and numerous arrests. People were strongly discouraged from joining the protests by aggressive police tactics, which saw police for the first time in Melbourne fire rubber bullets to control protestors.[58]

The penalties for failing to observe the laws were also significant. The main sanction that was utilised to deal with breaches of the restrictive directions was an infringement notice, which carries a fine which can be enforced through criminal law sanctions. The fines were, by any measure, large. The penalty for playing tennis or golf, fishing, mowing a neighbour's lawn or being 5.1 km from home during a Melbourne lockdown was $1,817[59] (and $5,452 for breaching gathering restrictions in the home or outside)[60] if dealt with by way of infringement notice, or over $20,000 if the matter is dealt with by a court.[61] There was no attempt to match the seriousness of the crime to the harshness of the penalty. The Victorian government seemed to be simply plucking sanctions from the air and hence violated the proportionality principle, which requires a matching of the seriousness of the conduct with the harshness of the penalty (and which the High Court of Australia has stated is the main consideration in setting penalty severity). As the High Court of Australia stated in *Hoare v The Queen*:

> ... a basic principle of sentencing law is that a sentence of imprisonment imposed by a court should never exceed that which can be justified as appropriate or proportionate to the gravity of the crime considered in light of its objective circumstances.[62]

The fines had a crippling impact on many Victorians and their families. Often the fines issued were far higher than the quoted $1,817. For example, a small family-owned mobile repair shop was issued with a fine of $27,261 in November 2021 because a (Covid-free and symptom-free) worker was not fully vaccinated. This would crush the business and imperil the financial stability of the family. It was draconian.

People were fined more than $1,000 for playing tennis.[63] A tennis court is 260.9m^2 and the players are separated by a physical net. The court was outdoors. The health recommendation is that to avoid the spread of Covid people should be separated by 1.5m. There is not a single case anywhere on earth of Covid transmission as a result of playing tennis. Fining people for engaging in manifestly healthy activities such as playing tennis is not a sign of a normal functioning society; it is the opposite of that.

If people cannot or do not pay Covid fines, severe enforcement processes can be activated. *Fines Victoria* can obtain an enforcement warrant allowing the sheriff or police to detain or sell the person's car. Also, the sheriff can enter the person's home and take items to sell to pay the fine and even sell a person's house. If the person has nothing which can be sold, the money can be taken from a person's wages or Centrelink payments. As a last resort, the sheriff can arrest people for non-payment of fines and if they do not work the fines off through community work, a magistrate can sentence the person to jail.

It is not in doubt that there was a need to have legal mechanisms in place to deal with the tiny fraction of people who callously disregarded health protocols and wantonly put other people at risk of being infected with Covid. However, there are already criminal law offences that prohibit this conduct in the form of offences that make it illegal to engage in conduct that places or may place another person in danger of death or serious injury.[64] There was no need to subject people to criminal penalties when they had simply made innocent oversights and had no desire to spread Covid.

> Legislators and other authorities … must exercise restraint and caution when creating and employing criminal offences, not only in the context of COVID-19. …[T]he use of criminal law and punishment must be the very last – not first – resort.[65]

The harshness of the pandemic criminal laws was exacerbated by the manner in which they were enacted. An indispensable aspect of the rule of law is that laws must be publicised and knowable. A unique aspect of Victoria's pandemic laws is the rapidity with which they were enacted and enforced. Melbourne often went into lockdown with less than 24 hours' notice.[66] The legal instruments which imposed the lockdown restrictions were sometimes published after the lockdowns were imposed (i.e., after midnight on the day in which they took effect); meaning that it was literally not possible for individuals to understand the scope and nature of the restrictions which had been imposed.[67]

Even Premier Andrews was issued with a Covid fine – for failing to wear a mask.[68] In one respect this can be regarded as demonstrating the integrity of the Covid laws by showing that no person was above the law. But the more compelling message is that the laws were effectively impossible to habitually observe, and a degree of judgement needed to be applied in enforcing the laws. Few people in Victoria were more informed about the nature of Covid and its spread than the state's premier. He repeatedly conveyed this message to all Victorians and yet even he slipped in complying with the laws. This highlights the immense difficulty that all Victorians faced in, first, understanding the laws and, secondly, in meticulously complying with them. In short, with only a hint of exaggeration, it was not humanly possible to always comply with every Covid law.

The integrity of the criminal law response to Covid was further diminished by the fact that there was no method in place to properly review and cancel Covid fines in circumstances where the breach was trifling or inadvertent. A review by *Fines Victoria* stated the internal police process for reviewing Covid fines was inadequate because the criteria that were applied for reviewing these fines were not adapted to the subject matter. Incredibly, the review noted the criteria that were utilised to review Covid fines were cut and pasted from traffic camera review guidelines. The Review noted:

> The [Traffic Camera Office] Guidelines appear to have been developed specifically for traffic offence reviews reflecting that fines for traffic offences are issued and reviewed within a clear legislative framework under the *Road Safety Act 1986* and are generally 'strict liability' offences, with the physical elements of the offence generally established conclusively through the evidence obtained from road safety cameras.
>
> COVID-19 fines are issued in a more complex legislative framework.
>
> The Review accepts that a COVID-19 offence involves a significant risk to public safety, however review officers should not be guided by guidelines that appear to have been developed for

> road safety offences as they are different to COVID-19 offences. For the avoidance of doubt, the guidelines for internal reviews of COVID-19 fines should direct review officers to have regard to the specific circumstances raised in the application.[69]

In reviewing the appropriateness of Covid fines, no account was taken of matters such as the nature and purpose of the conduct which resulted in the pandemic fine, whether the conduct was deliberate or accidental, or the likelihood of the conduct endangering health.

Jurisprudential failures of the pandemic laws

The pragmatic shortcomings of the pandemic criminal laws were underpinned by serious jurisprudential failures. The criminal law is the strongest means of condemnation in our society. In order for an act to be deserving of blame and the deliberate infliction of punishment, it should breach some type of moral norm or cause harm to another person. It has been accepted for over a century that, as observed by Lord Coleridge in *R v Dudley & Stephens* (1884), "the absolute divorce of law from morality would be of fatal consequence".[70] Lord Devlin later argued that one of the main objectives of the criminal law is to maintain and enforce public morality.[71] Hence, it is inappropriate to criminalise normal behaviour and subject citizens to criminal punishment for conduct which is not morally flawed. As has been noted previously:

> Because of the severe implications for human rights and civil liberties, criminal law measures are the *ultima ratio* that can only be utilised in the most severe circumstances and only if other, less intrusive means are proven to be non-effective.[72]

It is for this reason that criminal guilt normally requires a guilty mind. This can be constituted by a number of different mental states, most typically an intention to break the law or a reckless disregard for the law in question. In rare instances, crimes can be committed through a high degree of negligence, for example inadvertent driving which results in the death of a person.

Accordingly, the criminal law has traditionally been reserved for dealing with the most damaging forms of human behaviour, such as violence, sexual assault, and theft. There is a need to maintain a connection between criminality and harm and subjective wrongdoing. A transient oversight which causes no tangible harm is not a basis for holding a person criminally responsible.

Yet, this is precisely what occurred with Victoria's Covid responses. Even the most trifling, unintentional breaches of health directions resulted in people committing criminal offences. As noted above, the unfairness of this was exacerbated by the fact that often the laws which imposed the restrictions were unknowable because they were only released on the internet after midnight on the day the laws came into effect.

The severance between personal culpability and liability for pandemic breaches underlined the illegitimate nature of the pandemic laws.

How Andrews undermined the perceived legitimacy of his own laws

Research has previously demonstrated that there is a correlation between the perceived legitimacy of a law and the extent to which it is observed.[73] People are less reluctant to follow laws that they believe are unjust. To this end, unfairness comes in two forms. First, the rule itself is arbitrary or unjustified. Second, the punishment can be disproportionate to the seriousness of the conduct. As we have seen, the Victorian pandemic criminal laws failed on both these fronts. There is some evidence that violating these theoretical principles undermined the perceived legitimacy of the laws so far as the response by some members of the community is concerned.

By mid-2022, more than 50,000 Victorians had been issued with criminal fines for breaches of regulatory norms.[74] Not surprisingly, a large number of the fines have not been paid.[75] A report in June 2023 showed that only about 10 per cent of Covid fines had been paid in full.[76] A state government estimates hearing revealed that 50,150 pandemic fines which were issued totalled more than $100 million. Of these, approximately 5,500 were paid in full, 3,500 were paid and 14,319 were unpaid.[77] Approximately 4,000 fines were challenged in court and 11,800 were cancelled.[78] In total, the Victorian government had recouped $9.36m from the Covid fines paid in full.[79]

It has been argued that the ongoing and continued enforcement and prosecution of Covid infringements will continue to damage the relationship between the police and the community, and exacerbate the counter-productive impact of these laws.[80]

The overly punitive response to Covid restrictions also damaged the relationship between Victoria Police and the community. A survey by Roy Morgan in late 2020 found that the community's confidence in Victoria Police plummeted after police started enforcing Covid restrictions.[81] The survey found that only 42 per cent of Victorians rated the honesty and ethical standards of Victoria Police as either high or very high, a stark drop from 76 per cent three years earlier.[82] The survey noted that police actions during the pandemic significantly contributed to this decline.[83] Comments by respondents included: "We've seen some disappointing incidents of police brutality recently", "Head stomping, pulling people from cars, raids on people's houses for Facebook posts", "Too heavy handed, I have lost trust", and "They behave like they are above the law. For the first time ever, I'm scared of the police". This final comment was from a respondent aged over 65.

Many police members also became demoralised as a result of the enforcement of Covid restrictions. In October 2021, Acting Senior Sergeant Krystle Mitchell resigned after 16 years in the Victoria Police, stating that enforcing the Covid restrictions troubled her greatly and that she and most other police did not believe it was appropriate to enforce the restrictions.[84] She stated:

> There was a big thought process and battle of morals and integrity within me about what I wanted to do and how I see my organisation being used during this pandemic and it troubled me greatly. … But behind that is all of my friends that are police officers that are working the front line and are suffering every day enforcing

> CHO directions, that certainly the great majority don't believe in and don't want to enforce. ... I'm choosing to quit because I can't remedy in my soul any more the way in which the organisation I love to work for is being used and the damage that it's causing to the reputation of Victoria Police and the damage it is causing the community.[85]

Thus, there is evidence that some members of the community viewed the pandemic criminal laws as being unfair and illegitimate. However, the overwhelming message is that most Victorians were not greatly alarmed by the overly punitive laws being imposed on their lives. At the time the laws were enacted and enforced there was not a huge community outcry against the laws but, to some extent, this is attributable to the fact the Victorian government made it unlawful for people to protest during the period of the pandemic.[86]

However, what is even more indicative of the general acceptance of the pandemic criminal laws is that the community re-elected the Andrews government shortly after the pandemic finished – in November 2022 – and with a net gain of one seat. Of course, there are many issues upon which elections are fought. It is not possible with confidence to isolate the impact that any one issue had on the overall sentiment of voters. Thus, it may be the case that many voters strongly disagreed with the criminalisation of pandemic restrictions, and the length and severity of the lockdown, but these did not sufficiently trouble Victorians to punish the Andrews government at the polling booth.

Perhaps the most surprising and revealing attitude to the pandemic criminal laws was the total acquiescence to them by the human rights industry. Victoria was the first jurisdiction to enact a human rights charter,[87] and is regarded as the most rights-embracing state or territory in Australia. Yet, the groups and individuals which are normally the most vocal when it comes to asserting the importance of human rights went missing during the longest Covid lockdown on earth. It is evident from this that human rights in Victoria are mainly political concepts that are expediently invoked by public interest groups to criticise policies and practices by Liberal governments, as opposed to being universal moral standards. Paradoxically, the most vocal critic of the pandemic criminal laws was the Institute of Public Affairs, which has traditionally opposed human rights charters. Instead, it remained true to its core ethos of prioritising the virtues of liberty and individual freedom.

Conclusion

Throughout his time as premier, the criminal law was a key instrument employed by Daniel Andrews to regulate the lives of Victorians, from political communication, rights of expression and association, and private religious practices, to imposing the strictest Covid lockdown in the world. The criminal law is society's harshest means of condemnation and strongest instrument of coercion. It must only be used as a last resort for serious wrongdoing. Imposing criminal sanctions on Victorians for engaging in banal, everyday activities which are permitted in even the most dictatorial of societies – such as sitting in a public place, being out after dark, playing sport, and congregating with more than two people – is the greatest overuse of the criminal law in a democracy in recent history.

The criminalisation of Covid restrictions was reflexive, unintelligent, and damaging. It was ruthless. It traumatised everyday citizens, pitted police against the community, and violated key rule of law virtues, including the principle that laws must be knowable and transparent. The response was pragmatically unworkable, and most fines remain unpaid.[88] It was jurisprudentially flawed. Incredibly, in the midst of the lockdown the human rights industry refused to criticise the overreach of the criminal law.

Alarmingly, the Covid period exposed the hollowness of Victoria's commitment to the rule of law and the absence of genuine checks and balances many Victorians assumed would have operated to moderate the development of authoritarian policy. The lasting legacy of the Andrews era is that while rule of law virtues can be trashed in less than a decade, it will take much work over many more years to reintegrate these principles into the state's institutions.

4

All eggs in one basket: The deliberate undermining of Victoria's energy security

Kevin You

Victoria's energy policy under Daniel Andrews' premiership was the manifestation of an old idiom: 'to put all your eggs in one basket'.

Under Andrews, Victoria began the process of an energy transformation, the driving force behind which was one fundamental goal: the monopolisation of the energy grid by wind, solar, and their peripheries, such as lithium batteries and green hydrogen.

This has gone hand in hand with the demonisation of other sources of energy, such as coal, gas, and nuclear.

Net zero by 2045 and the rapid transition to wind and solar

In an act of incoherent one-upmanship, the Andrews government responded to the already artificial and controversial net zero emissions by 2050 target adopted by other governments with its own target of net zero by 2045, as well as a mid-term emissions reduction target of 75 to 80 per cent (of 2005 levels) by 2035.[89]

This has contributed to the state facing an energy reliability gap as early as 2024.[90] The Australian Energy Market Operator's (AEMO) 2023 *Electricity Statement of Opportunities* (ESOO) report identified a "higher forecast occurrence of low wind and high demand conditions in Victoria, resulting in higher forecast reliability risks".[91] The document went on to warn:

> Many new wind, solar, battery, and pumped hydro developments have advanced sufficiently to be considered in the 2023 ESOO, however **solutions which orchestrate and coordinate consumers' generation and storage devices to support reliability have not yet demonstrated success at significant scale.** (Emphasis in the original.)

AEMO warned that "imminent and urgent investment is needed" to generate more electricity across the national electricity market, especially in Victoria".[i] This meant that Victoria gambled with the risk of blackouts, yet again, because of inadequate firm energy supplies.

This was the outcome of the Andrews government's approach to energy, and energy security, over the course of almost a decade. The only other state in a similar predicament according to the ESOO report was South Australia, which has already decommissioned all its coal-fired generation units and is now entirely reliant on other states for baseload power.[92]

Upon the release of AEMO's report, Federal Energy Minister Chris Bowen was confronted by ABC Journalist Sarah Ferguson on *7:30* about the issue of energy reliability—to which he replied that Australian households should rest assured because federal and state governments have a magic band-aid solution up their sleeves to deal with the chronic issues plaguing the energy market. He responded:

> We have existing schemes with very large industry users already, where AEMO asks large industrial users to moderate their use [of electricity] at various times. That's always been the case … and that will continue.[93]

---

i The national electricity market is a series of interconnected electricity networks that serve the states of NSW, Victoria, Queensland, South Australia and Tasmania.

In other words, the solution provided by the political proponents of variable renewable energy is that Australia should reduce its manufacturing capabilities and productive output when it runs out of energy.

The minister was correct to suggest that demanding manufacturers slash their output to accommodate the failures of net zero would not be unprecedented. Alcoa's Portland aluminium smelter, on the southwest coast of Victoria, had to pull back its production in June 2022 because the national electricity grid was unable to cope with the net zero-induced underinvestment in coal-fired generators. At the time, the Institute of Public Affairs (IPA) responded by releasing the following public statement:

> As the obsession with unreliable renewables continues to push reliable and affordable baseload power generators off the grid, electricity supply to large customers is becoming increasingly precarious …
>
> Without reliable and affordable energy, Australia will never have the sovereign manufacturing capability to produce the vital goods we need to operate and defend ourselves as an advanced, first-world nation.[94]

The emergency event of 2022 was not the first experienced by Victorians and other Australian households connected to the national electricity market. This was a repeat of an emergency load-shedding order, made by AEMO back in 2019 – which was also directed at Alcoa.[95]

Both emergency orders resulted from increased demand from electricity users in the midst of baseload power facility outages subsequent to the sudden decommissioning of the Hazelwood coal-fired power station in 2017. The repeat of the first order, in 2022, signified policymakers' inability to learn the lessons of the previous crisis. The circumstances surrounding these crises will be discussed in further detail later in this chapter.

The wholesale price implication of the two emergency events, both of which were felt hard in Victoria under Daniel Andrews' watch, is illustrated in Chart 4.1 below. The chart tracks movements in the quarterly average wholesale spot prices of electricity per megawatt hour in the Victorian electricity network. [ii]

The chart clearly shows that higher power prices and greater price volatility have become a feature of the Victorian electricity market since the last time Victoria decommissioned its coal-fired power station, in 2017.[96] The energy policies of the Andrews government were critical to introducing and entrenching higher prices and greater price volatility.

Chart 4.1: Quarterly average wholesale electricity price in Victoria per MWh

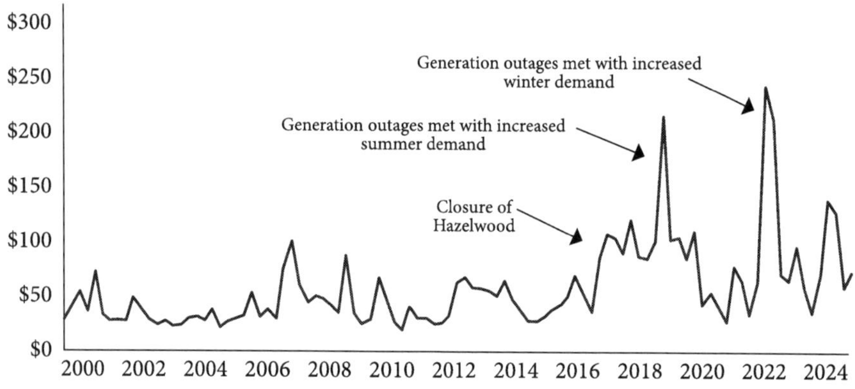

Source: AER, IPA

But the price hike and volatility arising from the reduction in baseload power is not the only challenge that Australia's energy market has had to face. The influx of highly volatile renewables being plugged into the electricity network will cause considerable damage to existing infrastructure unless the electricity market undergoes substantial upgrades by way of the installation of facilities such as synchronous condensers, storage mechanisms, and stronger interconnectors between state networks.[97] Much of this will have to be done through government mandate and at significant cost to Victorians by way of increased taxation and a prevailing shadow of uncertainty hanging over households and businesses.

ii A megawatt hour is a unit of electricity that describes the volume of energy produced by a power plant. Australia's annual electricity consumption is approximately 245 terawatt hours, which equates to 245 million megawatt hours.

Historically, Victoria's public institutions had placed reliability and affordability front and centre of their approach to energy supply and generation. This was upended by the Andrews government, which was focused on propping up wind and solar, and undermining other forms of energy generation to reduce competition. An outcome of this policy was to disincentivise private sector investment in sectors other than renewable energy generation.

The accelerated decommissioning of Latrobe's coal-fired power stations

The Andrews government's race to net zero resulted in the underinvestment of capital in coal-fired electricity generation units and the acceleration in the decommissioning plans of Victoria's coal-fired power stations. The passage of the *Climate Change Act 2017* (Vic), which legislated the state's net zero target, coincided with the closure of the 1,600 MW Hazelwood coal-fired power station,[iii] after which wholesale electricity prices spiked by 85 per cent and serious concerns were raised about the future of Victoria's electricity grid.[98]

Victoria currently has three coal-fired power stations remaining, all located in the Latrobe Valley. These are: Yallourn, Loy Yang A, and Loy Yang B. Combined, the three power stations can provide more than 70 per cent of Victoria's electricity needs. The rest is to be provided by a combination of gas power stations, hydroelectricity generators, and onshore wind and solar facilities.

iii A megawatt (MW), in this context, describes the size of the power plant in terms of its maximum capacity. A 1,600 MW power station has the maximum capacity, under ideal conditions, to produce 1,600 MWh of energy over the course of a 60-minute period.

Chart 4.2:
Victoria's annual electricity output by fuel between FY2000 & 2024 (GWh)

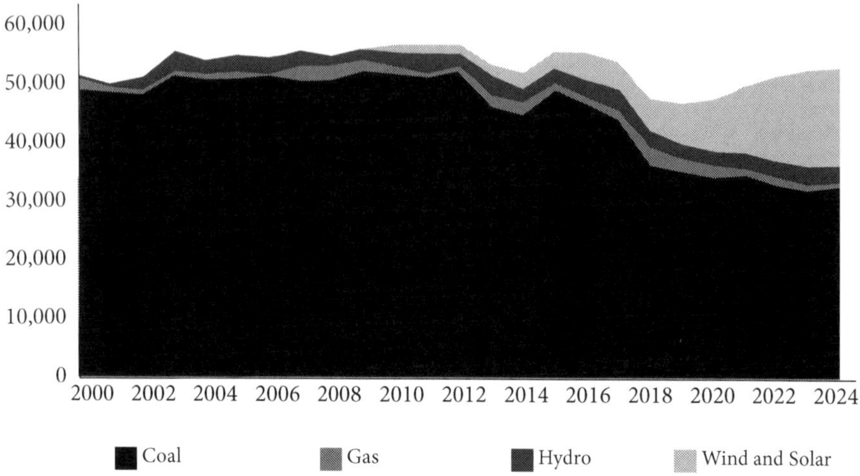

Source: IPA, Open Electricity

All the coal-fired power stations in Victoria are powered by lignite, also known as brown coal. Lignite has no export value and is plentiful in the state, mostly in the Gippsland, but also to a lesser extent across the Murray and Otway basins. This – and Victoria's historical gas reticulation requirements – was the reason energy had generally been cheaper and less volatile in Victoria compared to other states like New South Wales, Queensland, and South Australia.

Victorian energy prices were cheaper and less volatile especially in the years prior to Hazelwood's decommissioning. But the transition to renewables is forcing lignite-powered baseload power plants to close early.

Yallourn, a 1,480 MW facility which provided 22 per cent of Victoria's electricity, was meant to close in 2032. Under Daniel Andrews, its closure was brought forward by four years to 2028.[99]

Loy Yang A, a 2,210 MW facility which provided 30 per cent of Victoria's electricity, was meant to close in 2045. Under Daniel Andrews, its closure was brought forward by ten years to 2035.[100] IPA research estimated that the closure of Loy Yang A will see household electricity bills rise by 21 per cent. And it may cause the loss of 1,000 jobs in the Latrobe Valley alone.[101]

Loy Yang B, a 1,200 MW facility which provided 20 per cent of Victoria's electricity, was meant to operate well beyond 2047.[102] But this was inconsistent with the Andrews government's target of having 65 per cent of electricity sourced from renewables by 2030, and 95 per cent of electricity sourced from renewables by 2035.

Alinta, which operates Loy Yang B, has been put under considerable pressure to shut down its operation decades earlier – by 2035. Alinta's Chief Executive Officer, Jeff Dimery, was given no more than 30 minutes' notice before the government announced to the public that it would effectively force Loy Yang B to shut down by 2035.[103]

It should be noted that even the baseline dates for closure of these power stations noted above were notional, based on initial estimates of engineering life. They do not take into account the possibilities for life extension in a supportive policy environment. As IPA Executive Director Scott Hargreaves, has observed:

> Governments are putting definite timelines on closures, which means generators are starved of capital for maintenance and refurbishment, while they pursue pie in the sky projects at indeterminate delivery dates, putting system security at risk.
>
> The shills for the renewable lobby put propaganda into action by relentlessly working the phrase 'ageing coal-fired power stations' [but] like "Grandpa's Axe", refurbishment would mean the life of such stations could be extended for decades. Even, perhaps, in time for the only real base-load alternative, nuclear energy, to come online.[104]

Table 4.1: Coal-fired power generators in Victoria

	Yallourn	Loy Yang A	Loy Yang B
Owner or administrator	Energy Australia	AGL	Alinta
Nameplate capacity	1,480 MW	2,210 MW	1,200 MW
Commissioned	1974	1984	1993
Planned decommissioning	2032	2045	2047
Revised closure date	2028	2035	2035

Source: Energy Australia, AGL, Alinta

IPA research has shown that, historically, for every gigawatt's worth of coal-fired capacity removed from the national electricity market, wholesale prices jumped by approximately $22 per MWh.[105] The effect of the decommissioning of Hunter Valley's Liddell power station on the mainland section of the interconnected grid supports the finding. The removal of Liddell's remaining 1.5 GW generation capacity from the national electricity grid in April 2023 increased wholesale prices by an average of $33 per MWh, consistent with the IPA's study.[106]

The decommissioning of all three of Victoria's coal-fired power stations by 2035 will risk wholesale power prices increasing by well over $100 per MWh – doubling Victoria's electricity prices from June 2023 levels. In addition, as AEMO has already warned, it will jeopardise the state's energy security as variable sources of electricity (i.e., wind and solar) increasingly dominate the energy mix and replace firm generation capacity and output.

This is not mere speculation. As noted earlier, Victoria has already experienced two historic price hikes, after Hazelwood's decommissioning in 2017, which resulted from insufficient baseload power following a surge in demand for reliable electricity. The first was in early 2019, when a unit of Loy Yang A experienced an unexpected failure while, at the same time, a generation unit in Yallourn was out of action. Other firm capacity generators interstate, such as (the now decommissioned) Liddell in the NSW Hunter Valley and the Tallawarra gas plant on the shores of Lake Illawarra, also happened to be out of action – and therefore unavailable to ramp up electricity production.[107] Aside from Victoria, South Australia, which depends entirely on imports for baseload power, was also severely affected.

The second crisis occurred in 2022 when, again, a surge in the demand for reliable supplies of electricity coincided with an insufficient supply of coal-fired power, as well as outages in generation facilities resulting from an underinvestment in a market in which capital has been directed increasingly towards wind and solar. This time, the crisis took place during an unusually cold winter, which left the Victorian network especially vulnerable. In this instance, one of Yallourn's four generating units went out of action while supply challenges also confronted interconnected markets interstate – such as the unexpected disruption at NSW's Mount Piper power plant.[108]

A net zero target and an energy policy that prioritises a rapid switch to renewable energy are detrimental to energy security because they disincentivise investment in baseload generation facilities (namely coal, given nuclear energy generation is prohibited under Commonwealth law).

In this environment, baseload generators connected to the energy network have to endure a financial loss during the intermittent periods when wind and solar swarm the grid. Baseload generators are further disadvantaged by the more than $15 billion per annum worth of subsidies to the renewables sector nationwide.[109] Finally, net zero casts a shadow of uncertainty over the future of fossil fuels. IPA research found that $274 billion worth of economic activity across Australia, involving or associated with fossil fuel projects, will be put at risk under the policy of net zero by 2050.[110]

The Andrews government's commitment to a 95 per cent renewable target by 2035 will effectively end baseload power generation in Victoria: a move that IPA Research Fellow Saxon Davidson has slammed as "completely unworkable and must be immediately abandoned, lest families and small businesses suffer the consequences further".[111]

The bedrock of the Andrews government's energy policy, however, was never energy security. Rather, it was wind and solar's domination of the energy market. This placed a target on the back of not just coal, but also natural gas.

The war on gas

Towards the end of the Andrews government, the premier and the Minister for Energy, Environment and Climate Change, Lily D'Ambrosio, launched a campaign to drive up statewide electrification, namely the process by which gas and gasoline appliances, machines, and vehicles are replaced by electric ones.

It is estimated that full electrification in Victoria will increase annual demand on its electricity network by roughly 13 TWh per annum by 2035 and 37 TWh per annum by 2050.[112] This represents roughly three quarters of the state's electricity consumption in 2024. The effect will be to amplify uncertainty and energy insecurity throughout the state and beyond and, again, increase energy prices.

The Andrews government wanted Victorian families to be the vanguard of this march towards electrification, and for households to lead businesses in bearing the brunt of the upfront costs involved in the process.

Up until the middle of 2022, the Victorian Planning Provisions mandated that new homes built in Victoria should be connected to the state's gas network.[113] The mandate was aimed at providing Victorian families with lower power bills by taking advantage of the state's rich gas basins, especially in the Gippsland and Otway-Bass regions..

In July 2022, however, the Andrews government decided to scrap this mandate under a plan to phase out the use of fossil fuels in Victoria altogether. The energy minister said at the time that natural gas – used by about three quarters of Victorian households – was "no longer the cheap fuel it once was".[114] She further asserted that scrapping the gas connection mandate was about giving Victorians a choice between full electrification and dual gas-electricity homes. Freedom to choose was of the essence.

Twelve months on, in July 2023, the government finally came clean. Full electrification was never about giving Victorians a choice. The announcement was made that gas connections will be banned in new homes and government buildings across the state starting from January 2024.[115]

The push for compulsory household electrification was just the latest in a series of regulatory assaults by the Andrews government on consumers of natural gas. In 2021, the Andrews government instituted a constitutional ban on fracking. This action locked up trillions of cubic feet of natural gas that would have been available to Victorians, and which would have contributed to the state's energy security for many years into the future.

According to Geoscience Australia, there is 19.2 trillion cubic feet of unconventional natural gas in the Gippsland Basin alone. IPA research has found that this would be equivalent to 879 million petajoules of energy, which could power every home in Australia for the next 94 years.[116]

The constitutionally enshrined prohibition on fracking deters investment in natural gas when more gas is needed more than ever.

State electrification mandates will further disincentivise investment in natural gas production. Nonetheless, the Andrews government went ahead with the gas ban anyway, despite energy experts warning that a rapid transition to renewables, let alone achieving a net zero target, cannot possibly happen without a massive expansion in gas investment. As former Chief Scientist Dr Alan Finkel noted in the *Australian Financial Review*:

> The future of gas is to provide peaking generation to ensure continuity of electrical supply during sustained periods of low wind and sunshine. Using batteries, overbuilding, and more transmission lines to cover these extremes will either be impractical or very expensive.[117]

Former Head of the Energy Security Board, Kerry Schott remarked:

> I'm perplexed how you can run a system on renewables and batteries when you could have weeks of rain and can't recharge your batteries, and wind droughts … You have to have gas. In due course you can move it to hydrogen, but you need gas peaking plants.[118]

But the Andrews government was intent on demonising gas.

Independent analysis by the IPA found that the full upfront cost of residential electrification could total $81,000 per household.[119] Factoring in the number of affected households in Victoria – the state with the greatest number of homes connected to gas – the total cost of statewide residential electrification could add up to $206 billion, or roughly $7.62 billion per annum to 2050.

Chart 4.3:
Market price of residential electrification, by component, per household

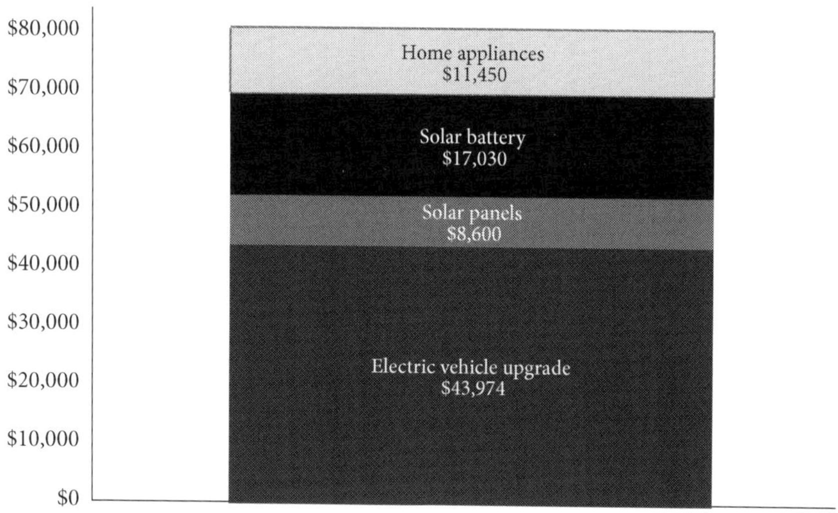

Source: IPA, Net Zero Australia

But that is not all. The Grattan Institute estimates that upgrading Victoria's electricity network to accommodate household electrification alone will cost another $11 billion.[120] This will include the one-off cost of the electricity network upgrade (or rather a series of upgrades throughout the network) plus the present value of the future costs of maintaining the expanded electricity network.

Table 4.2: Aggregate cost estimate of household electrification in Victoria

Cost component	Affected households	Aggregated cost
Electric vehicle upgrade	2,693,711	$118.45 bn
Solar panels	2,020,684	$17.38 bn
Solar batteries	2,707,734	$46.11 bn
Gas home appliances	2,089,000	$23.92 bn
Total		$205.86 bn
Annual cost to 2050		$7.62 bn

Source: IPA, PBO, Net Zero Australia, Energy Networks Australia

Moreover, despite advocating for electrification to meet emissions reduction targets, the Grattan Institute acknowledged that electrification in Victoria will in fact *increase*, not *decrease*, carbon emissions in the immediate term.

The combustion of each kWh of gas emits roughly 0.19 kg of CO_2-e.[121] In Victoria, electricity generation emits roughly 0.85 kg CO_2-e per kWh.[122] Nationwide, electricity generation emits approximately 0.68 kg CO_2-e per kWh of energy. Only in Tasmania, with its abundance of hydroelectricity, are emissions from electricity generation lower than 0.19 kg of CO_2-e per kWh.

Table 4.3:
Carbon dioxide equivalent emitted per kilowatt hour of electricity produced

Transmission network	Emissions from electricity generation
Tasmania	0.17 kg CO_2-e per kWh
South Australia	0.25 kg CO_2-e per kWh
WA (South)	0.51 kg CO_2-e per kWh
Northern Territory	0.54 kg CO_2-e per kWh
WA (North)	0.58 kg CO_2-e per kWh
NSW and ACT	0.73 kg CO_2-e per kWh
Queensland	0.73 kg CO_2-e per kWh
Victoria	0.85 kg CO_2-e per kWh
National	**0.68 kg CO_2-e per kWh**

Source: DCCEEW

Even accounting for the purportedly higher efficiency of electric stoves, ovens, heaters, and hot water tanks, household emissions in Melbourne would still be higher in an all-electric home (at 3.43 tonnes of CO_2-e p.a.) compared to a dual-fuel home (at 2.83 tonnes CO_2-e p.a.).[123]

The decision to deprive new Victorian households of a choice to use gas appliances seems at odds with an energy policy that – at first glance – has subordinated energy security, reliability, and affordability to emissions reduction. But emissions reduction had, in fact, been less of a priority for the Andrews government than securing the dominance of wind and solar in the state's energy market; in other words, to put all of Victoria's eggs in one basket: 'renewables'.

Daniel Andrews' State Electricity Commission

Renewable energy makes for a bad investment.[124] Renewable companies cannot compete fairly in the free market without heavy-handed government interventions. In Australia, this has amounted to more than $15 billion worth of government handouts per annum to the wind, solar, and related industries.[125] Wind and solar would falter without the financial support of taxpayers, as mandated and administered by those at the upper echelons of the political establishment. And the survival of renewables requires ever more direct government interference in the energy market.

On 15 June 2022, AEMO launched a takeover of the National Electricity Market because the policy of net zero had resulted in an energy crisis so severe it required an unprecedented level of government intervention. Subsequently, in the lead up to the 2022 state election, Andrews committed to reviving the State Electricity Commission (SEC) in Victoria, as a government-controlled entity in charge of electricity storage and generation. He also amended the state constitution to require a future government to obtain a supermajority in parliament should it wish to take the ownership of the SEC out of government hands.

The state-mandated switch to wind and solar became a preoccupation, with a commitment that, under the new SEC, "taxpayer funds will be used to guarantee returns for private companies looking to build massive wind farms off the Victorian coast".[126]

This is a far cry from the objective of the old, original SEC. IPA Executive Director Scott Hargreaves recalled:

> For those of us old enough to remember the 'original' SEC, it had as a key objective, 'a determination to achieve efficiency gains and to pass those on to consumers'. It was also committed to achieving commercial rates of return, and to deliver a safe and reliable electricity supply.[127]

The original SEC was established in 1921 and was chaired by Sir John Monash. It built on the work of its predecessor, the Victorian Electricity Commission (established in 1918) and was tasked with maximising the potential of the state's rich lignite deposit in order to free Victoria from its reliance on imported fuel. Doing so would entice private sector investment into the state by way of providing businesses with affordable and reliable energy.[128] The old SEC's earliest major project was the construction of the first Yallourn coal-fired power station.

In the 1990s, the Kennett government took the SEC to market and privatised the sector.

Daniel Andrews' new SEC was designed to be a very different organisation. Far from prioritising energy security, its focus is to facilitate the takeover of the energy sector by renewable operators. Far from delivering affordable and reliable electricity, it seeks to constitutionally entrench and exacerbate Victoria's energy crisis. Far from using the state's natural competitive advantage to deliver the energy needed to attract investment, create jobs, and foster economic growth, it will seek to undo the contributions that the original SEC made to the Victorian economy and the lives of Victorian families.

Shortly after winning the 2022 election, the Andrews government swiftly declared its new iteration of the SEC: a reorganising body under the *State Electricity Commission Act 1958* (Vic) and the *Electricity Industry (Residual Provisions) Act 1993* (Vic). This gave the new SEC the power to make its own decisions as a legal entity.[129]

Then Deputy Secretary for Tourism and Events at the Department of Jobs, Precincts and Regions, Chris Miller, was appointed as the SEC's interim Chief Executive Officer. And an expert advisory panel was put together, consisting of big names such as Dr Alan Finkel, former Telstra chief Andy Penn, and former AEMO chief Audrey Zibelman.

Less than a year later, the commission started to fall apart.

Dr Finkel – who, as noted, could not practically see a renewable transition without gas – walked away from the project. Benchmark power prices across Victoria rose by approximately 25 per cent on average. And the new commission struggled to find its very first project in the midst of what AEMO described as "a profound and recent slowdown in new financial commitments for large-scale user generation projects".[130]

"In fact, in the first quarter of [2023] there were no new financial commitments across the nation despite a strong pipeline of projects," according to AEMO's Chief Executive Officer, Daniel Westerman, as quoted in the *Australian Financial Review*.

By the time Daniel Andrews resigned as premier, and handed over the reins to Jacinta Allan, the new SEC had failed to even decide on its first project, let alone take solid steps towards delivering the promised 4.5 GW of renewable capacity to the grid. This was despite AEMO's warning of the critical importance of Victoria and other states connected to the national grid being able to secure "imminent and urgent" additional investment in energy generation if they are to avoid yet another supply crisis.[131]

The commission's initial budget of $1 billion was labelled "nothing but a stunt" by former premier Denis Napthine, who argued:

> We need a proper plan in terms of power supply. We need to continue using brown coal as long as we can, use gas, and look at nuclear, and we need to make sure Victorians have an affordable, reliable power supply.[132]

Scott Hargreaves regarded the new SEC as little more than a shiny new toy to boost Daniel Andrews' ego, which could not measure up to its original namesake:

> Rather than enhance energy security and local capability, [the new SEC] will be commissioning projects in which the turbines and blades are fully imported, almost certainly from China. Then we must hope that, in 25 years, which is the engineering life of an offshore wind farm, we can repeat the exercise and somehow pay for it all over again.[133]

The Grattan Institute's Tony Wood further questioned the adequacy of the SEC's budget, noting: "In today's world, you don't get much for a billion dollars ... There's so many unknowns and questions, and none of them have been answered yet".[134]

To suggest that the SEC can not only secure adequate replacement for the state's three remaining coal-fired power stations, but also play a key role in expanding the grid to support mass electrification and the switch away from gas is, plainly, wishful thinking.

The SEC *Strategic Plan 2023-2035*, published on 26 October 2023, is rich in motherhood statements and empty promises. Unlike Net Zero Australia's mobilisation report, which sets out – in glaring detail – how Australians must turn their lives upside down for the sole purpose of achieving net zero,[135] the new SEC's framing paper is a visual representation of the fantasy on which it was founded. The 48-page document sets out three priorities for the new SEC over the coming decade:

- Investing to accelerate the energy transition;
- Supporting the switch to all-electric households; and
- Building a renewable energy workforce.[136]

Significantly, it made no mention of energy security, and only vague and passing references to delivering affordable energy.

Conclusion

The Andrews government made Victoria's energy network more vulnerable than ever and contributed greatly to the cost-of-living crisis through which Victorians are suffering. At first glance, the Andrews government's energy policy seemed to have been driven by the desperate need to achieve a net zero emissions target. But the Andrews government's rejection of other sources of energy, which have the potential to greatly assist Victoria's transition to net zero, such as natural gas, indicated that net zero had always been no more than cosmetics.

For a government that has made many public commitments to diversity and inclusion, the premiership of Danial Andrews was anything but diverse when it came to energy policy. In fact, the Andrews government was dead set on placing all of Victoria's eggs in one basket: 'renewables'.

The long-term repercussions of Daniel Andrews' energy policy on Victoria are severe. Victorians risk ending up with an energy system that does not work. And given the Andrews government's proclivity to entrench bad policies into the constitution, walking away from such policies will be arduous.

But it is neither too late nor impossible.

Victoria still hosts three coal-fired power stations, fuelled by cheap and plentiful lignite. It is only after their permanent closure that the state's dependence on wind and solar will become permanent. The legacy of Daniel Andrews' premiership need not define the future of the state; but decisive action is needed now before it is too late.

5

The (mis)education state: Social engineering in Victoria's failing education system

Brianna McKee

After winning the 2014 election, Premier Daniel Andrews changed state number plate slogans to 'Victoria – The Education State'.[137] The number plate change was part of the state Labor Party's goal to make Victoria's education system the best in the country: "For as long as we can remember, number plate slogans have been part of the evolving identity of our great state," Andrews said. "Education is everything—it underpins the life opportunities and prosperity for families."[138]

However, over the course of his premiership, the state's education sector moved away from the core mission of transferring knowledge to the next generation. Instead, Andrews embarked on an aggressive social engineering project which entrenched ideological content in the Victorian curriculum and eroded parental rights. The policies pioneered in Victoria have now gained a national following – giving Andrews a legacy that extends beyond the state's borders – to the detriment of education nationwide.

Activism in the Victorian curriculum

The Andrews government's main achievements in the education space were ideological. During his time in government the state curriculum became increasingly political. Nowhere is this more evident than in the Victorian Certificate of Education (VCE) Australian History course for Years 11 and 12, which experienced catastrophic decline under Andrews. Between 2014 and 2022, the number of Victorian students studying the country's history has more than halved, from 1,245 to 478.[139] The downward trend continued despite the course being overhauled and a new syllabus implemented in 2022 to "revitalise the study for the next generation of students who are passionate about our nation's history".[140] This "revitalisation" was directed the study of history to politically charged themes of Aboriginal land management, race, immigration, the environment, and other challenges to "governing structures" such as union activism.[141]

For instance, one of the themes is titled "Power and resistance", which focuses on activist issues such as women's equality, demands for LGBTQIA+ rights, and Indigenous treaty debates. The purpose of this unit appears to be the indoctrination of students with a neo-Marxist system of thought, a lens through which history is viewed as a power struggle based on group identities such as race and gender. Students investigate how "the colonisation of Australia began as a complex story of the exercise of power and resistance to authority".[142] The 2022-2026 VCE History Study Design document states that the study of Australian History is considered within the context of "particularly Aboriginal and Torres Strait Islander peoples and culture" and "a colonial settler society", and teaches students that "the history of Australia is contested".[143] The obsession with race and colonialism evident within this syllabus is compounded by an emphasis on climate activism found within the theme entitled "From custodianship to the Anthropocene". Here students investigate "the way in which Australians' perspectives of the environment changed and/or remained the same after 1950"[144] by comparing Aboriginal land management to "colonisers and settlers [who held] different beliefs".[145] Ultimately, students enrolled in this subject will be left with a one-sided view of Australian history, one stripped of our nation's triumphs and leaving only the failures. The truly great achievements of the many explorers and leaders who have shaped this country, and the service men and women who defended it, will be sidelined by an activist narrative of oppression and colonialism.

English was another subject that suffered under Andrews. In 2020, a book titled *Required Reading: Literature in Australian Schools since 1945* argued VCE English was itself originally conceived as "a brave and imaginative attempt to develop an English curriculum that might challenge the bleak scenario entertained by [Marxist education theorist Louis] Althusser and others for whom schooling inevitably privileges the interests of social elites".[146] It was on these dubious foundations that the Andrews government accelerated the replacement of classics texts with modern texts, depriving schoolchildren of their cultural heritage as embodied in the Western canon. By 2024, more than half the VCE English texts that teachers had to select from promoted radical identity politics, and only six of the 36 options were drawn from the Western canon. As revealed by the Institute of Public Affairs, the complex new rules prescribing how texts are selected require at least two of the five texts students read to advance identity politics if teachers are to satisfy course requirements.[147]

Safe Schools, Respectful Relationships, and Doctors in Schools

Not only did individual subjects become more focused on activist issues. Broader Andrews government education policy focused on the communication of identity-based agendas and to undermine parental rights. Safe Schools came first in 2010, and much of this content made its way into the Respectful Relationships which was piloted in 2014-15 and formed the centrepiece of the government's social engineering agenda. Doctors in Secondary School was introduced in 2017 and was the most expensive of the three.

Safe Schools was funded and established by the Victorian government during the final months of the Brumby Labor government in 2010 and ardently supported by the Andrews government even when it came under fire for containing explicit content. While proponents claims Safe Schools was a benign anti-bullying programme that would help teachers foster a safe and supportive environment, it was revealed in 2016 that this "safe and supportive environment" entailed connecting students to pornographic websites, adult shops, and swingers' clubs. It was also linked to several alternative adult online communities and organisations that hosted hands-on sexuality classes. Students even received instruction on how to conceal their browsing history and were given lessons on chest binding and hiding male genitalia.[148] When the Liberals announced they would review the material following public outcry, Andrews was quick to hit back.

> The bad news is that the Liberals are still on the warpath about Safe Schools, a brilliantly effective program designed to stamp out bullying ... But, there is some good news. If the Turnbull government decides to cut the funding for this program, I'm proud to announce that the Victorian Government will make up the shortfall. We'll lock that funding in at the state level—because if it saves one life, it's worth it. Safe schools is officially saved in Victoria.[149]

The mission of Safe Schools, like Respectful Relationships, was to normalise the idea that gender and families are socially constructed. Roz Ward, a co-founder of the Safe Schools Coalition, admitted as much at a professional development session for teachers:

> Safe Schools Coalition is about supporting gender and sexual diversity... not about stopping bullying, about gender and sexual diversity, about same sex attraction, about being transgender, about being lesbian, gay, bisexual.[150]

Ward later argued at the 2015 Marxism conference that, "Marxism offers both the hope and the strategy needed to create a world where human sexuality, gender and how we relate to our bodies can blossom in extraordinary, new and amazing ways".[151] Her words suggest that Safe Schools was never about anti-bullying but rather, neo-Marxist indoctrination. This is important because Ward was not just a co-founder of the Safe Schools Coalition, but was, along with a team of staff at La Trobe University, contracted by the state government to implement the program itself. (The Department of Education now runs Safe Schools directly).

The Victorian government website misleadingly claims that Safe Schools is not a "compulsory part of the school curriculum". While Safe Schools is not a part of the state curriculum, it is effectively compulsory. Under the Andrews government all government schools were required to sign up by the end of 2018 with the only flexibility for schools being to decide what resources to use.[152] Safe Schools was protected and promoted in Victoria and much of its content has found its way into the Respectful Relationships programme.

From the outset of his premiership, Andrews championed Respectful Relationships. In 2016, he made it a core component of the Victorian curriculum and in 2024 it was included in the National Curriculum under the Health and Physical Education learning area. Despite being marketed as a family violence prevention strategy, Respectful Relationships functions as a Trojan horse for identity politics—teaching students to view the world through the prism of class, race, and gender. A teaching resource provided by the Victorian government lists three units of study. The first is titled "Gender, Respect and Relationships" and encourages the "deconstruction" of "masculinities, femininities and sexualities". Unit two is titled "the power connection" and explores "gender-based violence" with a particular focus on "homophobia". The third is titled "gender, power and the media" and covers "sexualisation", "pornography" as well as "gender and power".

This content, developed for the Victorian iteration of Respectful Relationships under Andrews, has been adopted by many states and territories and is taught to students across the nation. And given the nature of the topics covered, it is no wonder Respectful Relationships has been accused of exposing children to age-inappropriate content and seeking to disrupt and subvert cultural norms. For example, in April

2024 the education department was forced to launch an investigation after a Respectful Relationships presentation to year 9 girls included references to bestiality.[153]

The Doctors in Secondary Schools programme is the third arm of Andrews' ideological agenda in schools. It enables up to 100 Victorian government high schools to be visited by GPs on a weekly basis. Since its inception in 2017 there have been more than 72,000 consultations.[154] The reason this is problematic is the Victorian Department of Education's "Mature Minors and Decision Making" policy, which allows underage students to make decisions on their own behalf if the GP deems them sufficiently mature. This is clearly stated on the Victorian government website: "The GP will decide whether the young person is mature enough to consent to medical treatment or whether parent/carer consent is needed." This means that children can receive treatment for issues like abortion, sexually transmitted infections, and gender dysphoria without the knowledge or consent of their parents.

The initiative directly attacks the role of parents as the primary caregivers and therefore responsible for making decisions for their children. Instead, in the name of wellbeing, the Doctors in Secondary School program sees children become effective wards of the state, with the state having more rights than parents with regard to healthcare, and without transparency or due process. Revealingly, the state government even claims on its website that it is assuming this parental-like role to "reduce the pressure on working parents."[155]

Lockdowns and mental health

Any conversation about Andrews' education legacy must include the years of disrupted schooling during the Covid-19 pandemic. The lockdown measures gained the premier international fame, but not of the positive kind. Children in Melbourne were in lockdown four times longer than the average Australian and faced approximately 18 months of broken and remote schooling.

A November 2020 report by the Murdoch Children's Research Institute concluded the virus in children was generally mild and resulted in no symptoms.[156] Consequently, it was the indirect effects of the pandemic—academic, social and mental—that gave the most cause for concern. The report identified a lack of social opportunities, increased isolation, neglect and behavioural concerns as potential problems that would exist beyond the end of lockdowns. The report concluded that remote learning "should be a last resort".[157] However, nearly a year later Victoria was the last state in Australia to ease lockdown measures, including restrictions on schools.

Before the pandemic, students from disadvantaged backgrounds were the focus of various government programmes seeking to level the playing field. However, school shutdowns disproportionately impacted these students and especially those of non-English speaking backgrounds. Children from wealthier families were more likely to have educated parents who could facilitate learning at home, engage tutors, and afford better learning technology.[158]

Mental health was another problem exacerbated by Covid-19 lockdowns. A study published by *Lancet Public Health* found that while mental health had been trending down in Australia before 2020, there was a particularly large drop following the introduction of pandemic measures, and the decline in Victoria was twice as pronounced as the decline in other states.[159] More specifically, among children overall, mental health after the pandemic was more of a problem for 41 per cent according to the Royal Children's Hospital survey of national childhood health.[160] Anxiety was more of a problem for 36 per cent, and relationships more of a problem for 43 per cent. Despite returning to the classroom in October 2021, in December that year parents reported that 50 per cent of children still experienced negative effects on their mental health due to remote learning.

A study published by VicHealth in October 2021 found that people in Victoria aged 18-24 years experienced the highest rate of high psychological distress (23 per cent) compared to all other age groups.[161]

Another report, also by VicHealth, which surveyed people aged 15-29, found that loneliness increased in Victoria between April-June and July-December in 2020 but decreased in the other states.[162] During the second time period, Melbourne was experiencing a significant wave of Covid-19 infections and was subject to strict lockdown restrictions.

The academic and developmental problems caused by the extended stay-at-home mandates, curfews, and restrictions, continue to impact Victorian children. The government's multi-billion-dollar investment in education cannot even come close to undoing the effects of 18 months of intermittent education and the significant social dislocation of Victorian children.

Falling academic outcomes

It is a common, if counterproductive, strategy of governments to pump more money into failing programmes. Analysis by the Institute of Public Affairs debunks the assumed link between funding and education outcomes. The analysis found between 2012 and 2022 total state and federal government spending on school education increased by 43 per cent, while Australia's key OECD PISA results declined by three per cent nationwide.

Similarly, academic outcomes in Victoria under Andrews were in decline before the lockdowns, despite record funding. Unsurprisingly, years of disrupted schooling did not help. Since 2014, the Andrews government has invested $30.8 billion in Victorian schools. However, results appear to have plateaued or fallen in the last ten years, according to the OECD's 2022 Programme for International Student Assessment (PISA) scores.[163] According to PISA, Victorian school students in 2022 were 11 months behind where they were in 2003:[164] notably, no decline in the PISA scores were recorded between 2003 and 2015, whereas the scores recorded repeated declines between 2015 and 2022, the period coinciding with the Andrews premiership.[iv] Scores in scientific literacy

iv PISA is a diagnostic tool which evaluates educational systems by measuring between 2006 and 2022, and reading literacy between 2000 and 2022, have stagnated in Victoria.

The Progress in International Reading Literacy Study (PIRLS) test reinforces the PISA results. An international assessment of year four students, the PIRLS test is taken by 400,000 students from 57 countries. Following the Covid-19 lockdowns, Victorian students saw the largest fall in year four reading results across the country. The state's mean score dropped by 14 points between 2016 and 2021, and the number of students in the highest band of reading achievement decreased from 19 per cent in 2016 to 13 per cent in 2021, while the percentage of students below the proficient standard increased from 14 per cent in 2016 to 17 per cent 2021.[165]

Questions also remain as to whether the premier's record investment in schools was for the benefit of the teachers' unions or the students. During his time in office, Andrews was routinely accused of putting the interests of unions ahead of the community. It is true that many of the education unions supported the premier. In the leadup to the 2022 state election, the Australian Education Union (AEU) campaigned strongly on behalf of the Labor Party. Members were mobilised to attend polling booths in marginal electorates to distribute how to vote cards. In a statement, the AEU Victorian President Meredith Peace said "Putting public education first means putting the Liberals last" on ballot papers.[166] She promoted the Andrews government and condemned the records of previous Liberal governments. The AEU's campaign came just five months after the union worked with the government to broker an industrial agreement which featured a wage raise for teachers.

the performance of 15-year-old pupils in reading, science, and maths. Scores are scaled so that the OECD average is 500 and the standard deviation is 100. Research has shown that 25 points is approximately equivalent to one year of learning. Between 2003 and 2022, Victorian scores in mathematics declined from 511 points to 488 points, equivalent to students being approximately 11 months behind where they were in 2003. While there was no decline between 2003 and 2015, the scores dropped by 14 points between 2015 and 2018 and by nine points between 2018 and 2022.

The premier's close relationship with teachers' unions was especially problematic during the pandemic. This was because when many states were ending lockdown measures, Andrews sided with the education unions and refused to consider easing restrictions. His hardline position came under fire when it was revealed harsh measures, like the 8pm to 5am curfew, were not based on medical advice. Victoria's Chief Health Officer Brett Sutton admitted the curfew was not his idea, prompting federal health minister Greg Hunt to call for the curfew to be lifted. [167] However, Mr Andrews ignored pressure to ease restrictions and appeared to place the interests of teachers' unions and other pro-lockdown advocates before the community, exposing himself to accusations he was indebted to factional allies in the education sector. After the pandemic he came under fire for a $229 million package subsidising teaching degrees, which followed directly on the heels of a protest organised by the AEU where teachers and principals gathered outside state parliament. At the time, Andrews argued the timing was merely coincidental.[168]

Conclusion

More than ten years on from Daniel Andrews becoming Premier of Victoria in 2014, the state is filled with cars bearing 'the Education State' licence plates. But ultimately, his record in education is one of massive spending, a politicised curriculum, and declining results. Perversely, these failures have become the model for "progressive" education reforms nationwide. Daniel Andrews' legacy in education is to have fundamentally transformed the meaning of education itself; it now deals less with the transfer of knowledge and more with the transfer of divisive ideologies.

6

Unions empowered: Cost blowouts and delays in Victoria's public service and major projects

John Lloyd

The Andrews government implemented a radical workplace relations agenda that has had the effect of dramatically reshaping the state's employment system to institutionalise trade union power, with both the private and public sectors adversely affected.

Many employer and industry associations showed a marked reluctance to criticise the damaging changes. The Victorian Opposition has adopted a cautious posture. It is incapable of either generating serious debate about the nature of the changes or championing an insightful alternative policy. This is curious because those most adversely affected are small and medium sized business and their employees; a natural constituency of the Coalition.

This chapter canvasses the more egregious workplace relations changes. Common outcomes include increased labour costs, reduced competition, increased regulation and structural exposures that reduce the capacity of the Victorian economy to respond to future economic shocks. A particularly invidious culture has emerged in the Victorian Public Sector (VPS). The VPS has become an enclave where staff enjoy excessively generous entitlements and where standards of independence and professionalism have been compromised.

Background

The Kennett government in 1996 made the very important policy decision to refer the state's workplace relations powers to the Commonwealth. Agreement with the Commonwealth was reached in November 1996.

The change had risks. Victoria would be regulated by the Commonwealth. It became hostage to decisions and legislation emanating from the Commonwealth parliament. The Fair Work Commission was subsequently empowered to administer much of Victoria's workplace relations activity.

Victoria's influence on workplace relations policy and decisions was restricted. Its influence relied on the capacity to make representations to the federal government and its standing as one of the largest employers covered by the federal system.

Despite this, the Andrews government took several steps to regulate elements of Victoria's workplace relations system

The Andrews government, like all ALP governments, has extensive links to the trade union movement. The links between Daniel Andrews' socialist left faction and unions appear to be particularly strong. In an era of stringent limits on political donations, union leaders play a critical election campaigning role by getting out members to provide in-kind support.

The Victorian economy is weighed down by massive debt and high taxes.[169] A reckoning of such manifest economic mismanagement is inevitable. Victoria's capacity to deal with economic shocks is compromised. Adverse conditions such as low economic growth, high inflation and energy insecurity will affect Victoria more than other states.

Added to this mix is a toxic workplace relations culture where union leader insiders have won numerous concessions; concessions that, in particular, have delivered conditions of employment and entitlements that may prove unsustainable in the longer term. Productivity improvement, the only reliable pathway to rising living standards, was ignored by the Andrews government and union leaders.

In any workplace relations analysis of contemporary Australia, one compelling statistic stands out. Trade union membership has been on a steady decline for decades. In 2023, only 12 per cent of Australian workers belonged to a union. In the private sector only 8 per cent of workers were union members.

The union leaders' assumption of representing all Australian workers should be called out more frequently for the nonsense it is. However, the Andrews government and its union leader mates embraced this deception and the results have proven disastrous.

Construction - Melbourne Metro Tunnel

The Andrews Government immediately after being elected abolished the Victorian construction code. Move-on-laws aimed at controlling the use of blockades by unions were rescinded. Right of entry by union officials to work sites was made easier.

The construction of a large civil project or erecting a large commercial building in Victoria is an expensive undertaking.

In Victoria, large government civil projects proceeding under the banner of "The Big Build" are noteworthy for their cost blowouts and completion delays.[170] The Auditor-General's report into major projects performance comprises a list of more than a dozen major projects that have experienced "revised completion dates". And in a significant recent example, the Victorian Parliamentary Budget Office revised its estimate of the cost to build and operate the Suburban Rail Loop upwards by $16 billion from its estimate only a year prior, to a total estimated cost of $216 billion from 2019 to 2084.[171]

One key factor behind this astonishingly poor performance was the hands-off approach with the unions that has made exorbitant the cost of labour.

The construction unions, particularly the dominant CFMEU, is off the leash. The watchdog with teeth, the Australian Building and Construction Commission, has been removed.

Head contractors are faced with a left faction Andrews/Allan government and aggressive union leaders. The contracting firms' capacity to negotiate sensible enterprise agreements is limited. Sub-contractors on the big build projects simply cop what they are told are the terms and conditions that will form their enterprise agreements.

The earnings and entitlements that apply on the projects are extraordinary.

The example of a Traffic Controller is instructive. A Traffic Controller is the person who brandishes the slow and stop signs to control traffic flow in the vicinity of a site.

The Traffic Controller's basic remuneration has three standard components: a wage rate, a site allowance and a fares and travelling allowance to compensate for lack of parking at the site. The site and fares allowances are paid on rostered days off, even though the Traffic Controller does not attend the site on those days.

A Traffic Controller working at Melbourne Metropolitan Tunnel Project is paid $126,200. The three components are: wage ($94,500); site allowance ($17,900); and fares and travelling allowance ($13,800). Work on the tunnel can occur at night and on some weekends and attracts penalties of basically double time rates.

The contractor employing the Traffic Controller has to meet significant additional payments for the controller's work entitlements. These payments include: IncoLink redundancy fund ($160 per week, now double what it was as recently as 2020); income protection insurance ($31.50 per week); Cbus superannuation ($280 per week); training fund ($12.50 per week); welfare for families and apprentices ($6.00 per week); and long service leave fund ($49.00 per week). The payment of these mandatory entitlements adds a further $540 every week to the cost of employing a single Traffic Controller.

The training required to become a Traffic Controller is rudimentary, comprising a two-day course. Yet, the Traffic Controller earnings are high and markedly higher than most workers. The latest Average Earnings figure for Australian adults is $72,753. By way of contrast, the commencing salary for a registered nurse in Victorian public hospitals is $72,000 and for a state school teacher $78,000, both of which require tertiary qualification. The high pay for Traffic Controllers without any qualifications sends perplexing signals to the labour market.

A workplace relations system that produces such bizarre pay relativities will produce a labour market where incentive and reward misallocate labour resources. The wrong signals are sent to labour market entrants and participants.

In 2023, hardly a week went by without a report about the shortage of teachers and nurses in Victoria. These skilled jobs play a critical role in a modern and efficient society.

But why devote four years study for a nursing or teacher degree to then spend years trying to catch up to the earning capacity of an unskilled worker who chose construction?

This mess would be less damaging if construction in Australia and Victoria were highly efficient. However, commercial building and construction is a price setting activity with low levels of price and product competition. Its fundamental role in the nation's economic functioning should demand constant attention to productivity and efficiency improvement.

The reality is different. Agreements like that applying to the Melbourne Metro Tunnel Project make only passing references to productivity and efficiency in very general terms. More efficient work practices changes are typically kept off the negotiating table.

The current dominance of the CFMEU and fellow unions, aided by the Andrews/Allan government, will not end well. The cost of projects, particularly public infrastructure projects, is high and on a clear upward trajectory: In 2015-16, the state committed to 47 major projects at an estimated cost of $32.5 billion; by 2023-24, this had increased by more than 200 per cent to $99.5 billion across 128 major projects.[172] Taxpayers foot the bill and in Victoria's case endure massive debt for many years to come. Eventually, the ribbon cutting of new stations or tunnels will not hide the longer-term economic folly of the workplace relations jungle on big build projects.

Fire services

The signals from the outset of the Andrews government in 2015 were ominous.

The ALP in the 2014 election campaign promised to spend $140 million to recruit an extra 450 firefighters.[173] The United Firefighters Union (UFU) campaigned vigorously for the ALP, including the wearing of uniforms at polling booths.[174] The UFU, like any union, wanted improved pay and conditions. It also agitated for reform of Victoria's fire services, with an enlarged role for professional firefighters along with a reduced role for volunteer firefighters.

This agenda came to fruition with the Andrews government creating a new agency, Fire Rescue Victoria (FRV), in July 2020. The Metropolitan Fire Brigade ceased to operate. All operational Country Fire Authority (CFA) employees were transferred to the new FRV and the CFA model of integrated brigades was dismantled. Integrated brigades were split into two separate brigades: a paid firefighter FRV Brigade and a separate CFA Volunteer Brigade.

The lead up to this reform was painful and bloody for all involved.

An enterprise agreement was seen as a means to achieve many of the restructure proposals. The CFA Board and executive held serious reservations about the impact of the reforms on the organisation, particularly its volunteers. The transfer of too much power to the militant UFU was an underlying concern.

As an example of the state government's heavy-handed approach to workplace relations, the CFA Board was sacked by the government in June 2016. The CFA CEO Lucinda Nolan, a highly respected former police officer, resigned. The CFA Chief Officer and other senior officers also resigned. The Emergency Services Minister, Jane Garrett, also refused to support the proposed enterprise agreement, and resigned in June 2016.[175]

Worse though were allegations by Garrett that she was subjected to vile and personal abuse by UFU members. In 2015, video evidence showed Minister Garrett and Ms Nolan being surrounded and abused by firefighters when touring a fire station to promote increased female participation in firefighting. Ms Garrett complained that even as late as May 2021, five years after her resignation, she was still being harassed by bullies from the UFU.[176]

The first major industrial relations issue faced by the Andrews government sent a clear signal: some unions had a special relationship with Andrews and senior echelons of his government and the coercive behaviour of its members would not be constrained by the government. A minister or senior official who challenged or disturbed that special relationship placed their career in jeopardy.

In the midst of these changes the enterprise agreement applying to the FRV delivered substantial salary increases and extraordinary conditions of service. Leave entitlements are an example. Five types of leave reflect this outlier agreement that affords an employee up to 138 days leave a year.

The FRV workers enjoy some of the best conditions available to any worker in Australia. Also, the detail of the agreement represents a significant watering down of management prerogatives. Management is confronted with elaborate consultation and union agreement requirements that cover responsibilities like the ordering of new equipment and making submissions to the Government about planned legislative changes. This difficult management environment may be behind a Commissioner, appointed from overseas, leaving the job and returning overseas early in the term of their appointment.[177]

Change in workplace relations occurs regularly. That is the nature of the activity. However, there are many examples whereby change imposed contrary to the views of experienced people, ultimately fails to meet its objectives. The FRV second annual report of 2021-22 recorded a deficit of $133 million. The report blamed increased employee expenses associated with the new entity for the deficit. The FRV employed 4,500 workers and spent an average of $186,500 on each employee, including approximately $21,300 per employee on overtime.[178]

The fire services levy is a tax designed to provide reliable and adequate funding for Victoria's fire services. All Victorian property owners pay the levy that is collected through their local council rates. The fire services levy was estimated to raise $847 million in 2023-24.[179] The total expenses of FRV in 2021-22 were $1.1 billion.[180] It is hoped that FRV can in future achieve a better balance between the levy and expenses.

Volunteer firefighters are fleeing the CFA. Many are dissatisfied with the reforms and their treatment. It is reported that 10,000 have left since the Andrews Government came to office in 2014. Figures show that operational volunteers have declined from 38,335 in 2014 to 28,936 in 2023.[181]

The fire service reform has all the hallmarks of an astounding failure of public administration, particularly in its brutal execution. The IBAC is reported as conducting an investigation into the dealings of the Andrews government and the UFU. Lengthy legal battles have blocked the release of the final report.[182]

Portable Long Service Leave

The Andrews Government has taken several regulatory initiatives that advance and entrench interventionist union agendas. A new portable long service leave scheme for selected industries is a compelling example of this.

Long Service Leave (LSL) is something of a unique Australian employment entitlement. A worker who gave ten years continuous service to an employer was entitled to three months paid LSL. Inevitably, eligibility has been relaxed over the years and most employees with seven years' service have access to LSL.

The rationale behind LSL was to reward an employee's loyal service to an employer. It also worked as an employee retention device for employers.

LSL became an accepted industrial standard and is guaranteed by state acts of parliament and some modern awards.

Portable long service leave, based on service within an industry, rather than to an employer, emerged in the building and construction industry in the 1980's. This reflected the industrial strength of the construction unions and was supported on the basis of the "follow-the-job" nature of construction work.

The Andrews government and the unions saw an opportunity to enhance their appeal by extending the portable long service leave right to industries with high employee turnover and low trade union membership rates.

In July 2019, the Portable Long Service Benefits Scheme was introduced for workers in the community services, contract cleaning and security industries. It allows an employee to take their long service entitlement with them if they change jobs and stay in the industry.

Businesses must register with the compulsory scheme. Employers pay a quarterly levy into the scheme. Levy rates are 1.65 per cent or 1.8 per cent of an employee's wage. Employees are eligible for LSL after seven years.

Most employers, including those in these industries, make provision in their accounts for the firm's LSL liability.

The Andrews scheme contains a particularly egregious and unfair condition. Employers are not reimbursed if an employee leaves their employment. This could be defensible if the employee transfers to a new job within the industry. However, many employees will choose to work in another industry or country. The employer cannot recover the levy in these circumstances and the Scheme makes a windfall gain.

Employers can only seek reimbursement of the levy if the employee chooses to be paid by the employer pursuant to the Victorian LSL Act or a Fair Work Commission instrument.

Yet another government agency, the Portable Long Services Leave Authority has been created to run the scheme. The Scheme cuts across the original rationale for LSL. It is a clear additional cost on employers in the three nominated industries and contains demonstrably unfair conditions about reimbursement of employer levies. It will be no surprise if unions seek to expand the scheme to other industries.

Labour hire

Labour hire plays an important role in the modern Australian economy. Labour hire is used to access specialist skills a firm cannot afford to retain, and to provide labour during periods of surging work demand, for example during harvest.

Union leaders and the ALP have an intense dislike of labour hire. Labour hire workers, who number about 300,000, are not inclined to join unions. The workers generally value their independence from a normal employer-employee relationship and are confident in their capacity to earn a living without trade union nurturing.

The Andrews government, in April 2019, established the Labour Hire Authority, yet another government agency, to regulate labour hire. Registration with the Authority is required to operate legally as a labour hire business in Victoria. Host businesses must only work with registered labour hire firms.

Labour hire firms must comply with relevant laws relating to workplace relations, taxation, superannuation, Occupational Health and Safety, workers compensation, and migration, to be deemed "fit and proper". A licence is granted for a 3-year period. Labour hire firms must report on their activities annually. Severe penalties of up to $150,000 and $600,000 for individuals and businesses apply where a breach of the restrictive labour hire rules takes place.

The government's ostensible aim is to protect vulnerable workers from exploitation and underpayment. Exploitation is rare and recourse to legal and industrial remedies is available. The real agenda is to impose regulatory costs on labour hire employers, discourage this important economic activity, and to promote and expand traditional employment relationships that empower trade unions.

Victorian Public Sector

The Andrews Government's alignment with the workplace relations strategies of trade union leaders has had devastating impacts on the VPS. A fall in the quality and independence of the VPS harms all Victorians.

People who have worked in unions, as ALP staffers or with associated entities such a labour law firms and major consulting firms are favoured for appointment to senior VPS jobs and to the boards of numerous government agencies.

The VPS that employs 355,000 workers, has become a public administration that is extraordinarily compliant to the Government's agenda. Its compass for meeting its statutory obligations to be independent and impartial appears to have been lost. Accountability has diminished to such an extent that rarely is anyone held responsible for costly failures in policy and program implementation.

The VPS industrial malaise was highlighted during the Covid-19 Hotel Quarantine Inquiry, which heard evidence by a departmental official that the awarding of government contracts, in this case to a security firm, required the approval of the Victorian Trades Hall Council (VTHC) before a contract could be awarded.[183] A minister gave evidence to the inquiry that the practice of consulting the VTHC had been adopted in other areas of government policy.[184]

In other Australian jurisdictions third party scrutiny, let alone approval of contracts, would be regarded as a contravention of proper tendering practice. A tender would be pulled, an investigation of the contravention undertaken, and a new tender initiated.

Further evidence of the declining standards of the VPS is highlighted by the increased power of the public sector unions and the resultant generous leave entitlements of public servants.

Union membership in the private sector has fallen dramatically, to only 8 per cent of the workforce. The union membership decline has also been significant in the public sector, although not as dramatic as the private sector. This has meant that public sector union leaders have increased financial clout, representation and influence across union and ALP forums.

ALP governments, therefore, are more accommodating of public sector union agendas than in the past. The Andrews government has overseen a massive increase in VPS numbers and labour costs. Government-union negotiations on headline pay increases may be orchestrated to convey responsible outcomes. The reality of course is different and current staffing levels appear unsustainable.

The Andrews government has conceded substantial improvements to conditions of employment in the VPS. These concessions tend to escape detailed scrutiny.

One example is the leave entitlements contained in the VPS enterprise agreement 2020. The enterprise agreement sets out 27 types of leave, including gender transition leave (four weeks paid, 48 weeks unpaid), cultural and ceremonial leave (one day paid leave for NAIDOC, three days paid ceremonial leave), First Peoples Assembly attendance leave (ten days paid), sporting event participation (two weeks paid leave) and other leave for cultural or religious purposes.

Many VPS employees continue to work from home, notwithstanding the end of the pandemic. The Andrews government has been reluctant to demand higher attendance at the office. This facet of VPS employment adds to the difficulty of managing leave applications and entitlements.

The attempts of professional public officials to maintain proper standards of conduct have met with mixed success.

Expedient actions that serve the interests of ministers, politicians, their staffers and union leaders create situations of significant pressure for honest officials. The ethos of maintaining favour to achieve career advancement fosters opportunities to exploit compromised standards and to avoid proper process and accountability.

One such case was investigated by IBAC.[185] In February 2018, the Secretary of the Health Workers Union (HWU), began to lobby an advisor in the Premier's Private Office with a proposal for an aligned body, the Health Education Federation (HEF), to be contracted to develop and deliver occupational violence and aggression training for healthcare workers.

In May 2018 an advisor to the Minister for Health helped the HWU shape an unsolicited proposal that HEF be contracted to deliver the training. The advisor then submitted that proposal to the Department of Health and Human Services (DHHS) for consideration in June 2018.

Staff in DHHS had significant concerns about the proposal, including the capacity of HEF to deliver the program, and considered that there should be a competitive procurement process.

The Minister's Chief of Staff said that the Minister would be unhappy about being asked to approve either a direct grant to HEF or a competitive procurement process.

The 2018 State election was due to be held on 24 November. The 'caretaker period' for that election was to commence at 6pm on 30 October 2018. By convention, governments and their departments are required not to take action that may bind a successor government, such as entering into major contracts, during the caretaker period.

A DHHS deputy secretary authorised a non-competitive process in which only HEF would be asked to provide a detailed tender. HEF submitted a tender proposal, which was assessed by DHHS, resulting in the deputy secretary executing a contract for $1.2 million with HEF on 30 October 2018.

After the contract was signed, serious concerns were raised by DHHS about the standard of training provided by HEF under the contract. However, intervention in 2019 and early 2020 by an advisor in the new Minister for Health's office, at the request of an advisor in the Premier's Private Office (PPO), dissuaded DHHS from taking steps to terminate the contract.

The evidence to the Inquiry fell short of "corrupt conduct" as defined in the IBAC Act. However, IBAC found that it revealed breaches of the duties and obligations of ministers, ministerial advisors, and senior public servants. Senior public servants failed to meet their obligation to give frank and fearless advice to Ministers.

IBAC made 17 recommendations to ensure staff and ministerial codes of conduct are less opaque, and to crack down on advisors pressuring public servants.

Premier Andrews, when responding to the report, tended to downplay its importance. He noted that the staffers and Ministers identified in the report had left government service. He observed that the issues raised by IBAC were covered in "very broad, sweeping and undefined terms".

While this contract came to the attention of IBAC, it is open to conjecture how many additional contracts have been awarded without due process.

The processes for the awarding of contracts must be rigorous and beyond manipulation. However, an unwelcome workplace relations culture has developed in the VPS. Senior people with strong political connections are widely distributed. The standards of independence, political impartiality and professionalism have been undermined.

Moreover, the VPS has become a woke bastion where workplace diversity and inclusion is gospel. An example of the unbalanced attention afforded to woke notions is this extract from a departmental annual report:

> Through targeted initiatives and programs, action plans and celebration of significant days on the diversity and inclusion calendar, the department has further elevated its focus on the importance of diversity and inclusion. Our staff-led networks played a significant part in capturing the lived experiences of our people, strengthening intersectionality, diversity, and inclusion. These networks have also contributed to organisational strategies and action plans …
>
> In April 2022, a new Safe and Respectful Workplace Behaviours Policy and Safe and Respectful Response Procedure were released in a format under one Framework, the Safe and Respectful Workplaces framework.[186]

It is not readily apparent what all that means. But it does suggest there is thorough attention paid to diversity and inclusion. This is usually achieved by a well-staffed section found in the department's Corporate Services division.

Conclusion and future

The challenge for the future is what should be done to rectify the damage caused by the Andrews government. The Opposition and employer associations need to be more assertive about the economic harms caused, and must also vigorously prosecute a reform agenda that facilitates productivity, innovation, and growth. This agenda must be bold. Such an agenda will inevitably attract criticism from entrenched interests. Criticism seems to unsettle many of our politicians, but sensible policy will prevail.

7

Failure on every front: The economic legacy of Victoria's Covid-era decisions

Gigi Foster[v]

Under the Daniel Andrews premiership during the Covid era, Victoria became one of the most radical regimes on Earth. Personal liberties of movement and association were suspended en masse, schools and universities were shuttered, experimental medical interventions were mandated, and state propaganda was delivered daily by all major media outlets for years. The population was kept in a perpetual state of anxiety while normal economic life was suspended.

While Andrews has finally stepped down and media reports indicate that some in positions of authority during the Covid era have begun to express doubts about what was done,[187] the full social and economic fallout of Andrews' Covid-era regime has yet to be grasped by a population physically and psychologically abused under his authority for years. In this chapter I provide a high-level evaluation of the performance of Victoria during the Covid era, using several metrics

v Acknowledgements: This work benefitted from excellent research assistance provided by Michael Baker. All errors that remain are mine.

typically deemed relevant in the discipline of economics. On every front and on every metric examined, Victoria's record is execrable.

Evaluating the economic legacy of the Andrews government's Covid-era decisions

Regular, independent, public, and critical evaluation of government policy was never so necessary as during the Covid era, when states around the globe capitulated to their populations' media-fuelled panic about a novel respiratory virus. Instead of charting a calm, reassuring, and evidence-backed path towards the recovery of sanity and protection of health and wellbeing, the leaders of most Western governments embarked on the most radical and freedom-destroying peacetime policy trajectories seen in the modern era. To make things much worse, instead of welcoming critical evaluation of their decisions and nurturing public discussion and consideration of alternative policy options, those same governments weaponised the machinery of state and their connections in the private sector (including the media) to silence and denigrate those who spoke out against their radical policies.

In this chapter, I offer some of the critical evaluation that was rarely awarded a place of respect on the mainstream airwaves in Australia's time of need due to the monocular, censorious and bullying behaviour of governments, journalists, and even those in my own profession of economics.[188]

Thorough evaluations of Australia's lockdown response have now been publicly disseminated by courageous publishers elsewhere,[189] so in this chapter I focus on Victoria in particular – arguably Australia's worst example of a state-turned-tyrant during Covid. I proceed in the manner that would have behoved the state itself to proceed when considering the implementation of its radical Covid-era policies: by evaluating these policies against standard metrics of value and efficacy for the people of Victoria, whose interests the state is supposed to serve.

I begin by considering the narrow view of mainstream economics, in which monetary costs and benefits are the primary measures of interest, and broader measures of economic thriving are often seen as too complicated (or too contentious) to merit inclusion. I then move to a more comprehensive analysis of the impact of Victoria's Covid-era policies on human wellbeing, using the WELLBY currency that has come into its own during the Covid era as uniquely suited to capturing the costs and benefits of policies like lockdowns. Finally, I consider how the decisions made by the Andrews regime during Covid have impacted Victoria's reservoir of intangible goods – goods like trust, respect, faith, good habits, and optimism – which, while not usually accounted for in most policy evaluations, are crucial unseen inputs to long-run social and economic health.

Evaluation 1: Mainstream economic measures

The Victorian Treasury's 2023 report, *Victorian Budget 2023/2024: Doing What Matters: COVID Debt Repayment Plan*, provides the state's own perspective on the costs and benefits of the Covid policy regime through the traditional Treasury (i.e., economic, by which is implied primarily monetary) lens. The report states that the full package of Covid response policies cost $40.1 billion in total—or approximately 7 per cent of annual state gross domestic product (or gross state product) – of which $31.5 billion was borrowed, and that these funds were spent in order "to save jobs and save lives and to get through".[190] This objective is noticeably vague. What exactly were these monies spent on? Again quoting directly from page one of the report, "things like hospital equipment, protective wear, testing centres, testing payments, vaccination centres and business support". The goal of these expenditures is stated as "to safeguard the economy – and to prevent economic scarring that would have left a generation out of work". We are led to believe by these words that the benefit of the largely debt-financed Victorian Covid-19 expenditure package was the avoidance of economic catastrophe.

Did Victoria's expenditure during Covid times in fact avoid an economic catastrophe that would have come about due to the impact of Covid were it not for Victoria's Covid policies?

The economic costs and benefits of Victoria's Covid response

For the moment, let us assume that something positive was indeed achieved for Victoria by these policies. Taking this conservative approach, the first standard economics question is then: "was the benefit achieved by the state's Covid policies at least as large in magnitude as the costs of those policies, i.e., $40.1 billion?" Let us construct a rough estimate of how much benefit the state could potentially have achieved with these policies, purely from an economic perspective.

The most extreme policy enacted was lockdowns of the whole population of Victoria, and/or of all people in various regions. What are the benefits that these lockdowns could have delivered?

Australia was told by then-Prime Minister Scott Morrison shortly before the May 2022 elections that 40,000 deaths of Australians had been avoided by the "regime" of lockdowns and border closures, a figure that the mainstream press appears to accept (though Morrison's attempt to take credit for it is more controversial).[191] Suppose for a moment that this estimate is accurate, and suppose that the Prime Minister was referring to deaths caused by Covid, which seems to be the implication. According to the Australian Bureau of Statistics, the average age of someone dying with Covid in Australia from March 2020 to March 2022 was 83.3 years,[192] quite close to actual life expectancy during the Covid era.[193] To the Victorian Treasurer's point about avoidance of economic collapse being the source of the "benefit" delivered by Covid policies, we must then consider what fraction of Covid deaths would have occurred amongst people in working-age brackets during this time period. We might generously assume that all Victorians under 70 were contributors to the economy either via paid work or unpaid labour, such as caring for others. The ABS data show that of all actual Covid deaths during this two-year period, 17 per cent of the men and 13 per cent of the women were under 70 years of age. Applying these figures to the Prime Minister's estimate of counterfactual deaths, we can estimate the number of contributors to Victoria's economy who may have been lost to Covid without the state's Covid policy response, by means of the following calculations:

> 40,000 * .256 (as Victoria's population is roughly 25.6 per cent of Australia's) = 10,240 [averted Covid deaths in Victoria]

Of these 10,240 allegedly averted Covid deaths, it would be logical to assume that the same sex and age breakdowns would have pertained as was seen in actual Covid deaths recorded from March 2020 to March 2022. This implies that of the averted deaths, 58.5 per cent would have been men, and 41.5 per cent would have been women; and moreover that 17 per cent of the averted male Covid deaths would have been of prime age (under 70, generously) and 13 per cent of the averted female Covid deaths would have been of prime age (under 70). This yields the following generous estimates for the number of economic contributors whose lives, and hence economic contributions, were "saved" in the Covid period because of the state of Victoria's Covid policies:

> 10,240 * .585 * .17 = 1018 men [averted male "working-age" deaths in Victoria]
>
> 10,240 * .415 * .13 = 553 women [averted female "working-age" deaths in Victoria]

To put these numbers in perspective, the Victorian labour market consists of 3.5 million people, according to the state's own website.[194] This means that the number of contributors to the economy saved by Victoria's Covid response under this scenario amounts to approximately 0.04 per cent of the state's labour force.

Would losing 0.04 per cent of the state's workforce have created economic Armageddon? If we were to be very generous, we might attribute to the state's Covid policies the preservation of the GDP per capita created by these 1571 workers (1018 men and 553 women) in each year in which lockdowns occurred, or roughly $90,000 per worker per year = $141.39

million * 2 years = $282.78 million. This estimate of economic benefits is magnanimous for a number of reasons. One is the ironic fact that much of this "preserved" GDP was actually never created because of the government's own Covid countermeasures, which were paid for largely by debt-financed state handouts.

Even if we count all the counterfactual deaths implied by Scott Morrison and the Australian Bureau of Statistics as potentially contributing to overall stress on the economy, including the health care system – a total of 10,240 deaths in Victoria over these two years – this figure is lower than the total count of all Victorian deaths in a standard three-month period, according to the state's own figures.[195] This, combined with the obvious fact that many people dying of Covid were already likely to succumb soon anyway, given their advanced age and comorbidities, means that even if the Prime Minister was correct in his counterfactual deaths averted, Victoria would simply not have had an economic or health catastrophe in the counterfactual world that the PM envisioned. The economy would not have shuddered to a halt, and the health system, undertakers, and cemeteries of the state would have been able to cope without undue difficulty.

In sum, the "benefit" of the state's Covid response was not even in the same ballpark as $40.1 billion. Although one might offer an estimated economic benefit from Victorian lockdowns of $282.78 million during 2020 and 2021 based on the calculations above – giving rise to a cost-benefit ratio of approximately $142 of cost to each $1 of benefit achieved by lockdowns – the fact that even that modest benefit was prevented from materialising by the state-mandated lockdowns makes it difficult to take this estimate seriously.

What could have been done instead?

The Victorian Treasury tells us that the cost of the state's Covid response was $40.1 billion, and that this was a cost necessary for fighting a fearsome respiratory virus. More realistically, the primary threat to

Victoria's welfare during this period was not a new respiratory virus, but the panic that gripped the vast majority of the population. This observation begs the question: What would have been the ideal way for the government to have responded to the events of March 2020? In economic terms, what would the best counterfactual have been?

Job one for a benevolent government in a time of widespread stress and fear is to calm the population, reassure it, and support the development of resolute courage in the community to face whatever the threat is. This is true in wartime, in times of disease, and in times of economic devastation. As Franklin Delano Roosevelt said at his first inaugural address in the midst of the Great Depression, "the only thing we have to fear is fear itself – nameless, unreasoning, unjustified terror which paralyzes needed efforts to convert retreat into advance." One may disagree with his methods in the ensuing years, but on this point, FDR was correct.

Daniel Andrews and the leaders of his political and bureaucratic machinery could have sent messages to the Victorian population starting in March 2020 to counter the terror they were being led into by relentless scaremongering messages and viral imagery sent about the alleged threat of Covid without full context, initially from overseas but eventually also from home and within their own social media circles. He could have led a determined, calm, and reassuring fight over the ensuing two years against disproportionate fear, and he could have reminded people of the tried-and-true means of minimising health damage in the presence of a contagious infectious disease. He could have focussed state resources on people truly vulnerable to the disease, in aged care homes and within families, and pressed the importance of strengthening the immune system, taking standard hygienic measures, remaining calm and helping those who became symptomatic with known effective treatments for respiratory infections, such as vitamins, rest, sunshine, fresh air, and methods to reduce viral load such as airing out sick rooms and rinsing and gargling with saltwater. He could have formed a working group to monitor new approaches to treatment as they were discovered by the world scientific community, charged with converting this knowledge into actionable advice for Victorians, while making his approach transparent to voters and allowing natural immunity to develop amongst the young and healthy.

Such an approach, which would have been consistent with Victoria's pandemic management plans as they stood as late as 10 March 2020,[196] would have kept Victorians in work, supported the sick as needed, and avoided extra budgetary outlay. With no lockdowns, no fiscal support to families and businesses would have been required. The economic trajectory of Victoria might still have weakened due to the state's links with neighbouring states whose leaders might have succumbed to the madness – as happened to Sweden – but Victoria would have retained far more prosperity. Instead, in response to a stubbed toe, Victoria's leadership stabbed the state's economy in the stomach and then pretended that its treatment of that stab wound was necessitated by the stubbed toe, and that things would have been far worse without the stabbing. This pretence continues to this day. It is difficult to imagine a fairy-tale further from the truth.

The big-picture view

Another standard economic approach to assessing the costs of an action is to assess its opportunity costs. Specifically: what could Victoria have had for the $40.1 billion of funds spent largely on treating its self-inflicted stab wound?

That much money – 7 per cent of Victoria's gross state product (GSP) – could have financed any number of pro-human projects in the state, from building infrastructure to providing clean water to all rural and remote communities, to funding free home doctor services and cheap off-patent, effective medicines for vulnerable Victorians, to significantly upgrading the state's garbage disposal systems. Even building a new sports stadium (and following through on the state's commitment to host the 2026 Commonwealth Games)[197] would have been preferable to financing two years of state-wide suspended animation.

The $40.1 billion cost figure is an under-estimate even of the pure economic costs of Victoria's Covid response for many reasons. For example, it excludes the damage done by Victoria's Covid policies to other standard measures of economic health in the longer run, such as the inflation Australia has been experiencing for the past couple of years, missing workers,[198] and exacerbated wealth inequality.[199]

The Victorian Treasury *Doing What Matters* report calls the "global pandemic" a "one in one hundred year event". That statement is only true if by "global pandemic" is meant the destructive, fear-fuelled over-reaction to the virus that did indeed infect populations all over the globe. This pandemic of fear led governments, including Andrews-led Victoria, to declare states of emergency and use the power that everyone then assumed they had to compel everyone – infected or exposed or not – to stop working, stop attending schools, stop frequenting places of recreation or worship, and stay at home, notwithstanding the fact that not a single one of these measures had ever been proven to benefit humans in combatting a contagious respiratory virus, and all had been considered by scientific consensus to be off the table prior to mid-March 2020. It is this over-reaction that was a historical outlier – not the virus itself – and it is the over-reaction to Covid rather than Covid itself that caused unprecedented suffering for Victorians.

The leaders of the state of Victoria, including most importantly Premier Daniel Andrews, were not victims of an unprecedented virus from which they saved the people of Victoria. Rather, they were perpetrators of a degree of economic mismanagement unprecedented in peace time, on the politically seductive altar of "saving" Victoria from what was in reality a nasty flu. Victoria certainly needed saving, not from a flu virus, but from their leadership and indeed from their own fear. Instead of being cared for in their time of need, calmed and given actual help to deal with the arrival of Covid, Victorians were neglected, abused, lied to, and treated like imbeciles by their own government.

To see the enormity of these crimes, it is useful to adopt a currency far broader than just money.

Evaluation 2: Human wellbeing

In 2022, together with ex-Victorian Treasury economist Sanjeev Sabhlok, I published a cost-benefit analysis (henceforth "CBA") of Australia's Covid lockdowns.[200] For this analysis, I selected a currency in which to denominate both costs and benefits of Australia's lockdown policies with two core features: (1) it was capable of picking up damage to quality of life across a range of spheres deemed important to people, such that it could capture the intangible but intuitively obvious harms from policies like restricting people's freedom of movement and association; and (2) it was translatable to other known currencies, most importantly dollars and quality-adjusted life years (QALYs), such that costs and benefits whose native currencies were dollars or QALYs could be translated with ease, to enable apples-to-apples comparisons of costs and benefits. This currency is the wellbeing year, or WELLBY.

Introducing the WELLBY

The WELLBY, introduced to the world soon before the Covid era,[201] is built from answers to the following question that has appeared in near-identical form on social scientific surveys worldwide for decades:

> Overall, how satisfied are you with your life nowadays?

This question is answered on a 0 to 10 scale, where 0 is "Not at all satisfied" and 10 is "Completely satisfied". One WELLBY is one unit on this life-satisfaction scale enjoyed for one person for one year.

The average healthy person in a developed country like Australia typically answers around an 8 to this question, whereas someone suffering so much that s/he is indifferent between life and death will typically answer around a 2. Therefore, we can interpret six WELLBYs as effectively equivalent to the subjectively experienced value of one healthy year of life. For someone less healthy, or less happy for reasons unrelated to health, a year of life might bring fewer than six WELLBYs of value.

Subjective life satisfaction is arguably a reasonable proxy for what economists generally aim to maximise in their policy advice to governments. While we often devolve to targeting proxies of such a proxy, like GDP per capita, that is only because human thriving is known to be correlated with such second-level proxies. It is welfare, surplus, or total happiness that is actually our maximand.

In recognition of this, governments around the world have begun to adopt the WELLBY explicitly as the target of policy,[202] with assistance from the scientific community.[203] During Covid lockdowns, life satisfaction as measured through the WELLBY currency declined substantially,[204] which makes intuitive sense to anyone who paid attention to his community during a lockdown, and yet this is damage that would not be picked up by many other traditional economic measures. In my CBA of Australian lockdowns – which I presaged to the Victorian state parliament in August 2020, at the request of David Limbrick MP, in rough form[205] – both costs and benefits of the government's policies were estimated and expressed in WELLBYs. This choice allows us to determine how much greater the costs of the policies were than their benefits when we consider not only their direct monetary or economic costs and benefits, but their effects on a broad measure that is closer than any particular dollar figure to what people imagine when they think of the sort of life they want for themselves and their children.

WELLBY benefits of Victoria's COVID-19 response

In my CBA, I gauge the WELLBY-denominated benefits of Australia's Covid response by estimating, based on actual Covid deaths seen in countries around the world that enacted restrictions of differing stringency, the counterfactual number of deaths that Australia would have experienced had its leaders opted to enact a low level of restrictions on human freedoms during the Covid era. My coauthors and I document in *The Great Covid Panic* that countries enacting the tightest restrictions in 2020-2021 in fact experienced the highest daily counts of Covid deaths.[206] Nevertheless, in my CBA, I presume that some of the government's promised benefit from lockdowns would have materialised in Australia, and I take the higher of two plausible, data-derived (rather than simulation-derived[vi]) estimates for counterfactual Covid deaths. These estimates are drawn from the actual Covid deaths reported in countries with low levels of restrictions during the Covid era – namely Sweden, Belarus, Finland, Estonia, Taiwan, and Norway. After adjusting this estimate so it excludes actual Covid deaths experienced in 2020-2021 (i.e., those Covid deaths that Australian lockdowns failed to prevent) and is appropriate to the population size of Australia, my estimate of Covid deaths plausibly averted by Australia's lockdowns is 9,951.

If we assume that Victoria would have experienced a share of these deaths proportionate to its share of the Australian population, or about 25.6 per cent as of the 2021 Census, then the number of Covid deaths averted by Victoria's Covid policy regime would be estimated at around 2,547, which amounts to not quite one-quarter of the estimated 10,240 deaths averted based on the Prime Minister's claim of 40,000 people rescued nationally by lockdowns. For each such averted death, the state is estimated to have saved 30 WELLBYs, under the assumption used in my CBA that the average Covid death is of a person with five years of healthy life (i.e., 5 years * 6 WELLBYs per year) left to live.[vii]

Additional benefits of Victoria's lockdowns include averting long Covid cases occurring after initial 2020 or 2021 infections, and also

---

vi Much if not all of Victoria's Covid policy response was informed not by actual data, but by computer-simulated modelling interpreted by people blind and arrogant enough to believe that any human-built simulation could capture reality in sufficient complexity that basing unprecedentedly draconian, state-wide policies on its results was defensible. This is merely one example of the failure of science made evident during the Covid era: See Paul Frijters, 'From being to seeming: why empirical scientists failed in times of Covid', *Club Troppo* (Blog, 29 June 2020).

vii Even this is probably an over-estimate, since as at 30 September 2023, Victoria is reported to have lost over 5,000 people to Covid, potentially meaning that all of those allegedly "saved" from Covid by lockdowns, plus another group about as numerous, had succumbed to the disease within two years after lockdowns were lifted. Through this lens, what lockdowns accomplished was merely to kick the can (of Covid mortality) down the road. Australian Bureau of Statistics, *COVID-19 Mortality in Australia: Deaths registered until 30 September 2023* (27 October 2023).

a saving of life not originally offered as a benefit of lockdowns in the domains of fatal traffic accidents and homicides. In my CBA, I estimate the savings in terms of suffering due to long Covid to be valued at 2 per cent of the value of averted Covid deaths, and I estimate the savings due to homicides and traffic fatalities averted to amount to 131 people nationwide. Importantly, while Covid death on average afflicts those with few healthy years remaining yet to live, traffic fatalities and homicides affect far younger people on average. I assume that on average, a person who would have died in one of these ways in the absence of lockdowns had 50 healthy years yet to live.

Below I provide an estimate of the total benefit of Victoria's lockdown regime in terms of WELLBYs saved, applying the method used in my CBA and assuming population-proportionate fractions of losses for the state of the national estimates:

> 2,547 [Covid deaths averted by Victorian lockdowns] * 30 [WELLBYs per Covid death averted] * 1.02 [adjustment for long Covid suffering]
>
> +
>
> (131 * .256) [number of non-Covid Victorian deaths averted by Victorian lockdowns] * (50 * 6) [WELLBYs saved per averted non-Covid death]

= 77,938 + 10,061 = 87,999 WELLBYs saved in Victoria. At the 'exchange rate' between WELLBYs and QALYs that I use in my CBA, this benefit is roughly equivalent to 14,667 QALYs, because six WELLBYs equals one healthy life year, the definition of a QALY.[viii] This amount of human thriving would be worth $1.47 billion to Australia if we apply the rule of thumb, drawn from interactions that the Therapeutic Goods Administration has with pharmaceutical companies

viii The translation from WELLBYs to QALYs or dollars is not quite so simple as it may appear, since WELLBYs (as a broader measure of wellbeing) can be affected by things that cannot affect QALYs, and it is often cheaper to raise quality of life than to extend life. Nevertheless, the translations in this paragraph provide a ballpark estimate of the potential benefits of Victorian Covid lockdowns.

when deciding whether to add drugs to the Pharmaceutical Benefits Scheme, that our society is willing to pay $100,000 to save one QALY.

WELLBY costs of Victoria's Covid-19 response

The largest costs of Australia's response to Covid-19, when we evaluate these costs from a holistic human wellbeing perspective rather than merely counting money costs, arrived in two domains. The first was the direct damage to life satisfaction that occurred during lockdowns, which would not be picked up by traditional economic measures, and the second was a traditional economic cost: a combination of the hit to GDP (and hence the ability to spend on things that deliver human wellbeing) directly from lockdowns, plus the damage to future welfare from the debt-financed spending on JobKeeper and other Covid line items that will need to be repaid in future years, crowding out spending in those future years on line items that could (unlike debt repayment) have delivered human wellbeing. Additional areas of damage done by lockdowns to health and life satisfaction more broadly are numerous, including those associated with crowded-out health care, the development of bad health habits, disrupted education for school and university students, and the destruction of livelihoods.

In my CBA, I estimate conservatively – using data on actual declines in reported life satisfaction during lockdowns, and the economic costs of the lockdowns and the extra debt – that the total national costs of Australia's Covid response amounted to 23.41 million WELLBYs. Assuming that Victoria will have accrued only its population share of this amount – an assumption generous to the state, since in fact lockdowns and other Covid countermeasures were harsher in Victoria than in any other Australian state or territory – then Victoria's share of this lockdown cost burden would be approximately 23.41 million * 25.6% = 5,992,960 WELLBYs. At the exchange rates introduced above, this translates to 998,827 QALYs, or approximately $100 billion. This is more than twice the $40.1 billion of purely "economic" costs stated in the Victorian Treasury's *Doing What Matters* report, largely due to the direct human misery inflicted by lockdowns that is not captured if one tabulates solely monetary costs, as the Victorian Treasury does in its report.

Note that this total cost figure is not limited to costs felt in 2020 and 2021, but includes costs payable far down the road, not only due to debt repayment but also due to reduced health, reduced human capital accumulation, and reduced lifespans. Victoria, even more than her sister states and territories, traded off real human thriving tomorrow for indulging a disproportionate fear response today.

Comparing the estimated WELLBY-denominated benefit of Victorian lockdowns to the estimated WELLBY-denominated cost of these policies, we arrive at a cost-benefit ratio of 5,992,960/87,999, or 68:1. In other words, using the WELLBY currency and the method applied in my CBA for Australia's Covid response nationwide, the costs of Victorian lockdowns were 68 times their benefits, being conservative about costs and generous in estimating benefits.

Special mention is warranted of the costs to youth of these policies, which are included in the above aggregate figure. In my 2020 paper, "Early estimates of the impact of Covid-19 disruptions on jobs, wages, and lifetime earnings of schoolchildren in Australia", I estimate that the school closures Victoria enacted on 10 June 2020 resulted in a total of 36.8 million disrupted pupil-days of schooling for students from the preparatory grade through Year 12.[207] Using standard estimates of the returns to schooling drawn from the economics of education literature, and the assumption that a school day disrupted by lockdowns and held online instead of on-site would be 90 per cent as effective at developing a young child's potential as a regular school day, I calculated the foregone earnings of affected children due to these disruptions. For Victorian children alone, this figure was approximately $27 million. Subsequent to the analysis in that paper, Victoria implemented further disruptions to schooling that amounted to at least as many days of disruption again as had been included in the initial analysis, meaning that at least $50 million of foregone earnings of Victoria's schoolchildren was sacrificed because of the state's Covid response. Importantly, this estimate includes only foregone earnings due to lost human capital acquisition, without capturing the myriad other harms done to children's psychological, social, and physical health by keeping them out of school.

Evaluation 3: Impacts on intangible economic inputs

Apart from things like children's psychological and social health, many other stocks of economically and socially valuable intangibles were sacrificed in the Victorian Covid policy stampede, and not all will necessarily be picked up in subjective evaluations of life satisfaction during lockdowns. These include macro-level quantities like trust in our communities and our institutions,[208] and micro-level quantities like personal social confidence and trust in individual doctors who morphed during Covid from patient advocates into mere bullhorns for bureaucrats on pain of professional deregistration.[209]

Worsening the decay of Australia's social fabric, the anti-social corruption in many Australian industries only became worse during the Covid years, as documented in Murray and Frijters (2022).[210] A blatant example of the entrenchment of networks of favouritism is provided by a report released by the construction industry (Mundell 2023), in which it is shamelessly stated on page 2 that:

> The formation of an industry alliance (BIG1) comprising construction unions, employers' associations, and related groups was a critical success factor in the sector's continued operation during Victoria's multiple lockdowns… Presenting a united front increased the industry's lobbying power and access to senior government.[211]

One must infer then that those Victorian individuals and businesses unfortunate enough not to have been part of an "alliance" with "access to senior government" would have felt the full brunt of the government's anti-social Covid policy rampage.

Other intangibles negatively affected by Victoria's Covid response include people's motivation to work and their ability to derive meaning and personal value from that work, leading to further likely productivity stagnation; the collection of attitudes and soft skills developed by young adults when they attend university, TAFE, or apprenticeship programs (not to mention pubs and clubs) every day with peers; and the belief in a positive future that underpins decisions we make every day, itself a primary source of the "animal spirits" that John Maynard Keynes observed to be crucial to bustling economies.

A final word is in order about the Covid vaccines. The Victorian Treasury's *Doing What Matters* report explicitly mentions "vaccination centres" as one of the line items into which its Covid monies flowed, but notably it does not mention "pharmaceutical companies' pockets" in the same breath, probably because this would sound bad. Nonetheless, we know from the earnings of Pfizer and Moderna alone that tens of billions of dollars of revenue were earned from their vaccine products,[212] and further contracts were paid out by governments for various new anti-viral pharmaceutical products (such as Paxlovid) that these companies marketed to countries around the world.

While exact costings are hard to come by, mainstream reporting suggests that Australian governments will have spent at least a few billion dollars directly on vaccines, plus more for ancillary Covid healthcare products. Since the Victorian Treasury does not claim these expenditures in its report as part of the costs of its Covid response, one could argue it is fair not to claim any benefit from them that is specific to the state. This would be just as well from the perspective of painting a positive picture of Daniel Andrews' legacy, since if we were to tabulate the total human effects of the Covid vaccines, their net human benefit is likely to have been negative for a variety of reasons ranging from their poor efficacy[213] to their poor safety[214] to their needlessness for many of the individuals who were economically and socially coerced into taking them yet for whom Covid was a negligible health threat. Soberingly, I and my coauthors have recently estimated the maximum human costs of the Covid vaccines to be larger than any prior human-induced catastrophe.[215]

Yet even if one excludes the direct monetary costs of the mass Covid vaccination roll-out from the list of Victoria's ill-advised expenditures in the Covid era, one cannot in good faith exclude the patronising and denigrating deluge of verbal assaults on the Victorian population issued by Andrews and his coterie (including Chief Health Officer Brett Sutton) exhorting even healthy young people to get vaccinated against Covid, and backing up these exhortations with Covid vaccine mandates in many professions.[216] The pressure placed on every adult in the state to accept an experimental medical injection, just like the repeated directives over the course of two years that Victorians accept the medical experiment of population-wide lockdowns, directly violated principles of free and informed consent to medical treatment, and was in addition to regular urgings to socially distance, cover human faces in public, not watch sunsets,[217] and all manner of other ridiculous and unethical demands. For such crimes against humanity, perhaps Daniel Andrews and others who led Australia's despicable Covid policy regime will one day be prosecuted by the people of Australia whom they betrayed.

Summary and conclusion

Victoria's handling of the Covid crisis under the stewardship of Daniel Andrews was one of the worst examples of governmental incompetence, cowardice, bullying, destruction of the common wealth, and misallocation of resources that Australia has ever seen. It was truly a failure on every front.

What began as a nasty respiratory virus that prior generations would have viewed as no more than a minor hassle came to be held up as the reason for domestic abuse of the people by the machinery of state. Not only was Victoria's reaction to the arrival of Covid totally out of proportion to the actual health threat and hugely destructive – far more than Covid itself would have been, had the state simply followed its own March 2020 pandemic management plan – but state actors continue to this day to lie about what happened, painting their actions in a positive light and claiming that they saved Victoria from Armageddon.

In fact, due to the state's policies, the rich and connected got richer and more powerful while the poor and vulnerable suffered, and the state's stocks of human and intangible inputs to economic thriving have been significantly reduced. Even *The Guardian* newspaper is now publishing sobering analysis of Australia's economic losses and difficult road ahead,[218] with economic distress becoming clearly evident on graphs starting in the Covid era. As if the damage tabulated in this chapter were not enough already, the present scourge of excess deaths in Australia has yet to be explained by authorities,[219] with the most sensible candidate explanations being delayed lockdown harms and Covid vaccination side effects, both of which are direct results of government actions.

Rather than paying $40.1 billion on unproven "health" policies that damaged Victoria in the short run and the long run – to the tune of 68 dollars' worth of damage for every dollar of benefit generated by the government's actions – the Andrews regime could have spent a far lesser amount, proportional to the actual threat of Covid, on minimising human losses due to Covid using tried-and-true methods. The regime could have calmed, informed, and encouraged the population, protected the most vulnerable, left the economy alone, and translated into practical advice the best scientific information on early treatment and prophylaxis against respiratory viruses, including new ways to treat Covid specifically, as they were discovered and reviewed by scientists truly independent of large pharmaceutical companies. Had this happened, Victoria's population would have remained healthier throughout 2020 and 2021 and would have developed natural immunity far more quickly, and the need for a vaccine (with its costs and its dangers) would have evaporated, leaving the state with more money to spend on other, far worthier objectives.

With Daniel Andrews at the helm in the Covid era, Victoria was wounded by a self-inflicted gash whose full depth is still unknown, and that will take at least a generation to heal.

8

The China dream: Victoria's unprecedented foreign policy activities

Peter Jennings

In the history of Australia's federation, no state Premier has done more than Daniel Andrews to try to break Canberra's control of foreign policy. Andrews did this by seeking to build a partnership between Victoria and key Chinese central political institutions, all of which are directed by the Communist Party of China. An even more remarkable thing is that Andrews did this against substantial bipartisan opposition from Canberra, unhindered by oversight from his own Cabinet, largely avoiding federal and state public service advice, and hiding his activities from the media.

Daniel Andrews' China dream was to encourage trade and investment between Victoria and the wealthy, authoritarian People's Republic of China (PRC). Beijing would provide the economic engine for Andrews' ambitious but unfunded infrastructure plans, enabling his political focus on jobs and growth. China's leader, Xi Jinping, had his own China dream: to make his country globally dominant by 2050.[220] Achieving that dream required weakening the world's democracies and building economic dependence on China. What unfolded was a tale of Australian greed, naivety and stubbornness, manipulated by the PRC following its own strategic agenda.

Early dreams and a strategy

To be fair, in the first half of the 2010s, Andrews was not acting alone. The whole country from the federal government to the state and territory administrations, almost all our universities, and much of the 'top end of town' business communities were goggle-eyed with visions of Chinese money. On his victorious election night, 7 September 2013, Tony Abbott declared that his government was 'open for business'.[221] Much of what followed in the next few years showed that the most prized business target was the People's Republic of China. In an address to the Commonwealth parliament in November 2014, Xi Jinping spoke about the "comprehensive strategic partnership" that would flow following the just-concluded free trade negotiations.[222] Abbott declared, "We trade with people when we need them but we invest with people when we trust them. A relationship might begin with commerce but it rarely ends there once trust has been established, as I believe it has between Australia and China."[223]

Trade was booming. Xi told Parliament that two-way trade amounted to US$136.4 billion in 2013.[224] Chinese foreign direct investment was starting to grow, including via Chinese state-owned enterprises buying into Australian critical infrastructure such as the electricity grid and ports. Chinese fee-paying students had already become a central part of university business models. When Daniel Andrews made his first official visit to China as the Premier of Victoria in September 2015, the Australian mood was one of unquenchable optimism that China was the cashed-up answer to our national economic dreams.

The China-Australia Free Trade Agreement (ChAFTA) came into force on 20 December 2015. It seems clear that Andrews saw an opportunity. He wanted to position Victoria to become "the nation's Asian gateway – the place to go if you want to gain insight and get the deal done".

That was how the Premier expressed it in his foreword to *Victoria's New China Strategy: Partnerships for Prosperity*, released in April 2016.[225]

Like almost all Australian official statements about China from that time, the Victorian strategy is a mix of hope, hype, and half-truths. There was hope for uncomplicated investment streams which would fund the jobs and growth Andrews wanted for his state. The hype was evident in extravagant claims such as "Our cooperation will centre on the liveability of our cities. We'll be working together to build smart and sustainable cities for the next century." (That will surely raise a chuckle from visitors to grim, grimy, ghost-town Melbourne.) The half-truths should have been obvious even in 2016. The strategy claimed that Victoria's special partnership with China was "build not on transactions, but on trust and tradition". Was trust ever really that deep in dealing with Xi's China? Remember that 2015 was the year Xi went to Washington DC and openly lied to President Obama, claiming that Beijing would not militarise the South China Sea and that he would reduce intellectual property theft from cyber spying.[226]

Another statement clearly untrue in the Victorian strategy was that China "is transforming itself from a centrally planned and investment-driven economy to a market and consumption-led economy."[227] By 2016 it was clear that Xi was re-centralising China, reducing the scope for so-called 'privately-owned companies' to operate freely in the global market and driving the economy to deliver greater control for the Communist Party.

A core problem here is that neither the Victorian government, parliament, nor public service is equipped with the national security policymaking and intelligence apparatus to make accurate judgements about the capabilities or intent of foreign countries. Why should they be? As established in the Australian Constitution, the federal government is solely responsible for defence, national security, and foreign policy. From the start Andrews' China play was unburdened by the necessary knowledge, or responsibility, to really understand who they were dealing with in China.

Andrews was by no means alone in wishing for a different type of China to emerge from the growth generated by Deng's opening of the economy in the 1980s. Australian state governments, including Victoria's, had been assiduously cultivating relations with Chinese provinces and cities for years.[228] But what was increasingly clear at the start of the Andrews premiership was that China under Xi was becoming more Leninist, more authoritarian, more controlled, and more subject to the arbitrary direction of a single leader.

Nightmares begin to take over

Perhaps some of Xi's authoritarianism appealed to the man who himself came to be known as 'Chairman Dan', whose own leadership style became increasingly 'presidential'. What is clear is that, from around 2015-16, the federal government was ever more worried about the down-side risks of dealing with Xi's authoritarian system. In September 2015 the Northern Territory government leased the Port of Darwin to a Chinese company for 99 years.[229] The Port was (and remains) a critical defence asset in Australia's north. A loophole in foreign investment legislation exempted state and territory owned assets from Foreign Investment Review Board scrutiny. The Turnbull government scrambled to close the loophole but the Port of Darwin lease sparked national discussion about the strategic consequences of over dependence on the PRC.[230]

The risks of too much engagement with China shaped as a more serious federal concern. In August 2016 Treasurer Scott Morrison blocked a foreign sale of New South Wales "poles and wires" – the electricity transmission system – to a Hong Kong company and a Chinese government-owned enterprise.[231] In June 2016 a Chinese property billionaire, Huang Xiangmo, had offered Labor $400,000 to change its policy position on Beijing's annexation of the South China Sea. Only two weeks out from a federal election, Labor senator Stephen Conroy scotched the deal by publicly stating that a Labor government would resist Chinese encroachments in the South China Sea. Huang then turned to NSW Labor Senator Sam Dastyari. In Peter Hartcher's words: "Dastyari called a press conference and, standing side by side with Huang, said that 'the South China Sea is China's own affair' and that 'Australia should respect China's decision.'"[232]

In September 2016, Dastyari resigned from a shadow cabinet position after it was revealed that he had accepted payment from Huang to cover some legal expenses.[233] Dastyari then resigned from parliament in December 2017 after his South China Sea comments (originally given only to Chinese media outlets) became public. In 2019 the federal government cancelled Huang's Australian residency visa after ASIO found him to be a covert agent of influence for China. He was quoted in the Chinese Community Party newspaper, the *Global Times*, as likening Australia to being a "giant baby" and said: [ix]"I cannot figure out the logic of ASIO in regard to my efforts in promoting the reunification of China as threatening the national security of Australia."[234]

The Dastyari affair pointed to a substantial Chinese covert operation to suborn Australian politicians with financial donations, often from mysterious Chinese business figures recently resident in Australia. Between 2013 and 2015 Chinese-linked companies and donors poured over $5.5 million into the Liberal and Labor parties.[235] The Turnbull and Morrison governments strengthened legislation designed to prevent covert interference and otherwise strengthen national resilience. In 2017 the federal government declined a Chinese request to sign up to its 'Belt and Road' initiative[236] – a signature Xi Jinping initiative designed to promote Chinese infrastructure construction and funding around the world. Xi wanted countries to formally endorse the proposal through Memorandums of Understanding or other legal instruments. The federal position, endorsed by the Labor opposition, was that individual infrastructure projects would be considered but no political-level endorsement would be forthcoming for what was, in essence, a plan designed to entrench Chinese dominance in a global market for infrastructure development.[237]

The era of optimism and supposed trust between Australia and China was coming under strain. Beijing's overt and covert influencing, cyber spying, investments in critical infrastructure, its annexation of the South China Sea and undisguised pressuring of Pacific Island and Asian countries was rapidly changing how Canberra assessed the relationship. In August 2018, Huawei and other Chinese companies were excluded from involvement in the roll-out of the 5G network.[238] That led to angry public rebukes from Beijing. It was revealed that Beijing had unofficially cut ministerial-level political contacts with Canberra.[239]

This was the background against which Daniel Andrews continued to double-down on building closer ties with China. He kept his 2015 promise to visit China every year, going seven times as premier.[240] Andrews visited only five other countries during his premiership: twice to the USA, once to Japan and to Vietnam (as stop-overs on two China trips) and one trip which, oddly, took in Israel and Greece. It's clear that, for Andrews, China was the overwhelming international preoccupation. He kept spruiking the connection long after federal (and many state and territory) politicians had decided that some measured distance was the order of the day.

Aside from China's potential to spur Victorian jobs and growth through trade and investment, Andrews saw an opportunity in promoting the state's ethnic Chinese community as a central part of his plan to engage the PRC. He said in his foreword to the 2016 strategy, "the Chinese community has been a part of our community even before Victoria was a State".[241] True enough, but press-ganging Australians of Chinese ethnicity as part of a push to deepen engagement with the PRC was always a fraught proposition. Many Chinese Australians do not wish to be treated as "overseas Chinese" by the PRC, a label which dismisses the idea of Australian citizenship and assumes some 'paternal' oversight. Other Australians of Chinese descent may have ancestry from Taiwan or Southeast Asia and have no family connection to the mainland. Equally, many Australians with Chinese ancestry have direct family history and ties to China, but this is a diverse group of people and many are clearly not supporters of the Communist Party.

Why did Andrews make this 'ethnic relationship' such a core part of his strategy? Sumeyya Ilanbey, a business journalist for *The Age* and *Sydney Morning Herald* and author of an Andrews biography, hints at a possible insight. Andrews cut his early Labor political teeth organising Victorian ethnic communities. Ilanbey recounts his failed efforts to organise support from Turkish Australians for his then boss, federal Labor MP Alan Griffin. Much of Victorian Labor politics is about the politics of managing ethnic groups. In his maiden speech to parliament, Andrews declared "multiculturalism is not a concept or construct in my electorate. It is a reality. It is workplaces and neighbourhoods, classrooms and playgrounds."[242]

In his approach to the PRC Andrews was shaping a domestic political strategy as well – pitching for the Australian Chinese ethnic vote. To some extent this may have worked in subsequent state elections and in federal results in Victoria, but political parties make a dangerous mistake by treating ethnic groups as potential voting blocs, because it is individuals, not ethnic groups who vote. Treating Australians with Chinese ethnicity as a group whose votes are susceptible to how governments deal with the CCP overlooks the many different attitudes and motivators of these people and demeans their status as Australian citizens.

Andrews' 2018 Belt and Road Memorandum of Understanding (MOU)

In his assessment of the growth of the Victoria-China relationship, academic John Fitzgerald reports that leaders of China's Sichuan Province first proposed co-operation on the Belt and Road Initiative (BRI) with Daniel Andrews during his visit to the provincial capital, Chengdu, in September 2015.[243] For Chinese provinces and businesses, aligning with the BRI was a way to position for favour with the CCP hierarchy.[244] In late 2016 the China Investment Corporation invested $900 million into a share of a fifty-year lease of the Port of Melbourne.[245] On the face of it, Andrews' strategy to secure Chinese investment underpinning jobs and growth appeared to be working. What more could be achieved by aligning with the BRI?

In March 2017 Andrews signed an agreement with China's National Development and Reform Commission (NDRC). He Lifeng, as Chair of the Commission, was close to Xi Jinping and in charge of BRI projects. The NDRC invited Andrews to attend a major BRI forum for international Cooperation in Beijing in May 2017. Andrews' *Travel Outcomes Report* told Victorians that:

> I was the only subnational leader from Australia to attend the Belt and Road Forum for International Cooperation (BRF) in Beijing. ... This visit continued to build on the significant relationship we have fostered with China through my annual visits and Ministerial visits. ... China's positive global economic outlook and policy settings will continue to drive Victoria's trade and investment growth. There is a strong alignment between Victoria's strengths and China's development plans...[246]

China wanted international political support for BRI as a way of legitimising its global strategy to dominate transport and other infrastructure. In return for what looked like a constant stream of investment, tourists and fee-paying students, Daniel Andrews was prepared to provide that support, even at the price of going against the wishes of the federal Coalition government. The Coalition's *Foreign Policy White Paper* of 2017 warned that "There is a risk that trade and investment, which in the past have acted to restrain strategic rivalry, could fuel it instead."[247] It was a subtle but direct reference to the risks presented by the BRI.

Andrews formally 'signed up' to the BRI on 8 October 2018 with a Memorandum of Understanding (MOU) and followed that up with a 'Framework Agreement' on 23 October 2019. Both documents are vague on the details of what actions had been agreed. The MOU has a preamble that says: "the parties decide to work together to explore and form synergy in cooperation, enhance policy coordination, and further promote friendly cooperation."[248]

Article I of the MOU sets out "Objectives and Guiding Principles of Cooperation". It says the agreement will "seek new opportunities in cooperation and inject new momentum to achieve common development." Article II specifies areas of cooperation to "enhance policy cooperation, facilities connectivity, unimpeded trade, financial cooperation, people-to-people bond, and promote Digital Silk Road Cooperation." Article III on "Modes of Cooperation" predictably lists visits, dialogues, "joint researches, pilot programs, knowledge sharing, capacity building, etc." A fourth article says the parties will settle differences "through friendly consultations". Finally, Article V sets a date of entry into force (8 October 2018) and processes for amending and terminating the agreement.

Twelve months later the Andrews government claimed "Victoria and China Take Partnership to the Next Level" with a Framework Agreement that "will help fast track cooperation in the key areas of infrastructure, innovation, ageing, and trade development providing more opportunities for Victorian companies and more Victorian jobs."[249] Again, there were no specific projects outlined, but a Joint Working Group was to be established and co-chaired by Andrews and Vice Chairman Ning Jizhe of the NDRC to "guide and facilitate cooperation".[250]

One reaction to these documents might be to ask: 'what was all the fuss about?' There is nothing in the MOU or the Framework which specifies a single job or a single dollar of investment. However, it would be a mistake to dismiss the importance of the BRI agreements for several reasons. First, MOUs are intended to guide actions, not to list activities. They tend not to be specific. What counts is the intent of the parties to use them as platforms for action.

There is no doubt that Andrews intended that the MOU would shape real developments and he was making himself directly responsible for driving these outcomes. For example, after his May 2017 visit to China and Hong Kong, Andrews directed that the Victorian Public Service would work more closely with Hong Kong officials.

A July 2017 media statement declared:

> This first exchange of senior public servants has taken place this week with the Secretary of the Department of Premier and Cabinet, Chris Eccles, leading a group of senior Victorian public servants for a world first exchange program establishing direct policy collaboration.[251]

One should pause to consider just how astonishing this development is. By mid-2017 the Communist Party was well advanced in its objective to re-establish political control in Hong Kong, trashing the 1997 handover agreement between Britain and Beijing. Hong Kong's umbrella revolution began in 2014 championing democracy. In 2016 Beijing disqualified elected pro-democracy advocates from taking positions in the city's legislature.[252] Yet Andrews was pushing public service collaboration "to ensure Victoria's public sector remains equipped to solve complex policy challenges and keeps pace with world best practice."[253] At best this was a tin-eared assessment, at worst one which showed Andrews had not the slightest concern about aligning his administration with Chinese authoritarianism.

This highlights a second reason to be concerned about the MOU, which was that Beijing had a clear strategic objective, which was to create an impression of international endorsement for Xi's China and his signature policy, the BRI. Chinese officials and their supporters in Australia worked hard to deliver the MOU and Framework via a coordinated plan to influence Andrews and key business, public service and academic figures. Securing the Victoria-China MOU was a triumph for Beijing, the high point of an overt and covert political influencing campaign.

Third, Andrews' signature was a political prize that put the premier into Xi's corner when Canberra determined not to provide a blanket endorsement of the BRI. It seems that Andrews quite knowingly allowed himself to be wedged against Australia's own federal government. Beijing hoped this might weaken Canberra's resolve not to endorse Xi's signature project.

A fourth reason to regard the Andrews MOU as seriously concerning was that the federal government was itself worried. Based on intelligence assessments, allied perspectives and the direct experience of witnessing PRC covert and overt influencing attempts, successive federal governments had come to the view that the China 'risk' was seriously outpacing the China 'opportunity'. Managing national security risk is the prime task of federal government. On what basis was Andrews questioning that increasingly pessimistic assessment?

Tony Abbott's time as Prime Minister concluded at the time the Foreign Investment Review Board was discovering it did not have the power to intervene in leasing the Port of Darwin to a Chinese company. Turnbull started his premiership having been a businessman who had made substantial wealth in China, but his experience as Prime Minister and active interrogation of the Australian Intelligence Community had led him to take a more pessimistic view about Beijing. Scott Morrison as Treasurer and as Prime Minister saw first-hand just how abrasive, demanding and undermining the PRC could be.

Thanks to China's own behaviour, Australia was no longer open for business with the PRC by the time Andrews signed his MOU in 2018. The tragedy of Daniel Andrews' mismanagement of Victoria's China relationship was that Andrews did not consult with the federal government on the MOU other than superficially, did not seek intelligence briefings, did not even engage the wider Victorian public service in a discussion about the relationship. According to journalist Anthony Galloway writing in 2021 the Premier did not hand negotiation of the MOU to Victorian trade officials:

> Instead, Andrews ran the show out of his own office and department. The deal was kept a closely guarded affair, with Andrews and then-secretary of Department of Premier and Cabinet, Chris Eccles, intimately involved in the process. The jobs department, along with the then-trade minister Philip Dalidakis, were sidelined.[254]

According to biographer Ilanbey, Andrews "failed to consult with his own trade minister, the state and federal trade departments, and the Commonwealth. The saga highlighted Andrews' weak spot: a confidence in his own opinion that means he fails to seek and absorb advice."[255]

Dream weavers

Who did Andrews consult? An individual who seemed to have a major impact on Andrews' China policy was 'Marty' Zheng Mei. He travelled with the premier on all seven of his official visits to China. On the September 2015, September 2016, and May 2017 visits Mei is listed in Andrews' travel reports as a Multicultural Affairs Adviser. In the May-June 2018 visit Mei is listed as a Press Secretary and in the April 2019, October 2019, and March-April 2023 visits he appears as a Senior Adviser.

A May 2020 article in *The Age* by Eryk Bagshaw and Anthony Galloway reports that Mei came from the Hunan province in China and came to Australia in 2006: He "rose through the ranks of the Victorian Labor Party after leaving the Chinese state broadcaster CCTV. He joined Mr Andrews' office following the 2014 election after working for former Labor MP Hong Lim."[256] Mei is described as being instrumental in landing a $100,000 donation to the Labor Party before the 2014 election from Chinese-Australian businessman Jianping Fu.

Mei was also reported to be on the board of the Hunan Business Association. *The Age* continues: "The Hunan Business Association has links to the Chinese Communist Party's United Front department. The Chinese government has targeted independent community groups as a means of spreading its influence around the world." Bagshaw and Galloway claimed that: "Documents show while Mr Mei was the Premier's multicultural adviser, he was also a special consultant to another United Front-linked group, the Shenzhen Association. The association aims to promote stronger business ties between Shenzhen, China's Silicon Valley and Melbourne."[257]

The United Front Work Department refers to an agency in the Chinese

Communist Party focused on building support for the CCP among non-Party members in China and overseas. Strong under Chaiman Mao, the United Front has had a major resurgence in influence under Xi. In their study on the development of Xi's political thought, Tsang and Cheung note that the Chinese paramount leader puts particular stress on the role of "overseas Chinese" to be the Party's "eyes and ears" and to "tell the China story well". This means that "'patriotic overseas Chinese' are those who consciously apply themselves to the Party's United Front work, 'uniting every force that can be united, mobilising every positive factor that can be mobilised and gathering as much strength as possible to contribute to our [the Chinese people's] collective struggle'."[258]

A 2021 Lowy Institute report on Chinese community organisations in Australia found that: "The Chinese Party-state clearly reaches out to overseas Chinese communities in Australia to promote China's political interests and economic development."[259] The report found that there was a large-scale change in Australian Chinese community organisations in the 2000s, with younger individuals with business and Chinese Community Party connections taking over. "It is clear that Beijing's economic incentives appeal to some Chinese-Australians and are often promoted by community organisations."[260] In other cases United Front agents can intimidate and coerce community groups where willing cooperation is not forthcoming.

Interest in promoting China ties was by no means limited to Chinese lobby and community groups. The Australia China Business Council enthusiastically lobbied for the Belt and Road Initiative. Hugh White, a professor of strategic studies at the Australian National University, told an ABC conference in Darwin in 2017: "If you look at it from an economic point of view – and you look at the way it connects us with the Government's own plans for northern Australian development – it would seem pretty logical to sign up."[261]

In May 2016 an advisory group was launched in Melbourne to promote the connection with the Australia-China Belt and Road Initiative (ACBRI). Malcolm Broomhead, chair of Asciano and Orica and a director of BHP, was to chair the group. Broomhead told *The Australian*, "What makes this different from just rocking up to China with a proposal and trying to do business there, or with a Chinese company elsewhere, is that the financing has been specifically set aside."[262] The executive director of ACBRI was Jean Dong who, *The Australian* reported, has "a formal advisory role for the Victorian government".[263]

The ACBRI website biography of Jean Dong says that she had worked closely with the Tasmanian and Chinese governments on an agriculture MOU and, following that, established ACBRI as "a not for profit organisation" to "engage pioneering business leaders from China and Australia".[264] A member of the 2014 Australia-China Youth Dialogue, Dong's delegate profile claims that: "Prior to Jean's Australian journey, she enjoyed a rich experience as the editor of Youth newspaper (China), and a TV presenter and national reporter for CCTV television station (China)."[265]

The Australian reported in 2020 that Dong likely met Daniel Andrews though Mike Yang, who had been a staffer of Andrews in opposition and had travelled with Andrews to Beijing.[266] Like Marty Mei, Mike Yang worked for Hong Lim before moving to Andrews' opposition staff in 2011. A biography of Yang on the site of the 2014 Australia China Youth Dialogue claims that:

> Mike was a senior adviser to the Leader of the Opposition in Victoria on multicultural and China affairs between 2011 and 2013. He formulated and implemented strategies for the Leader of the Opposition and its shadow cabinet. In 2012 he planned and joined the Leader's first trip to China.[267]

According to John Fitzgerald, "Yang also helped to found the Australian Hubei Chamber of Commerce in which he served as inaugural chairman, and later served as a bridge between the Andrews' government and the local 'Chinese community'."[268]

In May 2017 Jean Dong claimed that ACBRI:

> "... was appointed as a consultant unit by the Premier of Victoria.

> 'The next step will be to assist the state government to sign a co-operation agreement with the National Development and Reform Commission and to set up the 'belt and road initiative' office. The centre will be responsible for planning and implementing specific projects, and strive to make Victoria a model for Sino-Australian 'belt and road initiative' co-operation.'"[269]

What emerges from these thickets of connections, organisations and individuals is that, at the time Daniel Andrews was pursuing his Belt and Road moment with China, many people in both countries wanted this connection to succeed. Beijing worked hard to promote its strategic plans and, by overt and covert means, reached out to Australian-based individuals to assist. And many Australians in business, universities and politics had their own reasons for pursuing closer engagement with the PRC, often because of perceived lucrative financial connections.

Wakeup call from Wuhan

The story of Dan Andrews' China dream takes a stumble following the unexpected but catastrophic arrival from the PRC of the Covid-19 pandemic. By early February Scott Morrison was preparing to ban flights arriving from China. Victoria was preparing its long and dark lockdown journey – one of the world's harshest control regimes and one that initially reinforced the Premier's dominant political position and his disregard for the institutions of democracy. Victoria's China policy took a backseat for most of 2020 while the state and the commonwealth dealt with the pandemic.

The national political impact of Covid was to harden the Morrison government's position against the PRC. Scott Morrison's entirely reasonable call for an international investigation into the origins of the virus produced a hysterical backlash from Beijing, perhaps most sharply expressed in the 14-point grievance list produced by the Chinese embassy in Canberra and handed to journalists in November 2020. "China is angry. If you make China the enemy China will be the enemy" an embassy official said.[270]

Perhaps not surprisingly this was a time when Beijing's domestic backers in Australia muted their support while the PRC unleashed a string of anti-Australian invective, trade bans, and suspension of political-level contact. The Morrison government enacted a law in December 2020 that required "states and territories, local governments and Australian public universities to notify the Minister for Foreign Affairs of existing and proposed foreign arrangements."[271] Over a thousand such agreements with foreign governments were reviewed. On 21 April 2021 Minister for Foreign Affairs Marise Payne announced that four would be cancelled, all involving the Victorian government. One was a 1999 scientific co-operation agreement with Syria and a second was a 2003 MOU with Iran on education. The third and fourth on Minister Payne's list was the Andrews 2018 Belt and Road MOU and the 2019 Framework agreement, "found to be inconsistent with Australia's foreign policy or adverse to our foreign relations".[272]

An oddly muted Victorian response just noted that "The Foreign Relations Act is entirely a matter for the commonwealth government".[273] Mired deep in his hard-line Covid response, Andrews perhaps knew the MOU game was up. As the Australian Constitution makes clear, it is the Commonwealth government which calls the shots on international relations. The state continued to boost relations with China even at a point when Beijing's unilateral trade bans were hurting Australian businesses. In October 2021, 'Vic House', a "new state-of-the-art trade facility", was opened in Shanghai.[274] The three-story building featured "rooms to conduct virtual business meetings with importers and retailers".[275] It added to Victorian trade and investment offices in Beijing, Nanjing, Chengdu and Hong Kong. The Andrews government reportedly "[covered] the costs of dozens of Victorian firms exhibiting at the most important annual trade event in China".[276] This contrasted with a federal government approach encouraging businesses to diversify markets away from China.[277]

Andrews made his seventh and final trip to China as Victoria's Premier from 27 March to 1 April 2023. This was the first visit of a senior Australian political figure in years. Accompanied by Marty Mei and Ben

Foster, one of Andrew's "inner-circle" staffers, the trip became public only days before it happened. Andrews declined to take media, saying "this is not very picture-friendly."[278] He also declined to raise human rights issues with his hosts, including about Victorian journalist Cheng Lei who, at that point, had been imprisoned in China for over two years on fake spying charges. In a rare concession to the Commonwealth's primacy in foreign affairs, Andrews conceded that Cheng Lei's case involved "deeply sensitive matters … best dealt with by the Australian foreign service".[279]

Five months after his last China visit Andrews resigned on 26 September 2023. In an interesting footnote to the Andrews premiership, the *Weekend Australian* reported in January 2024 that Andrews had established two businesses, although the documents lodged with the Australian Securities and Investments Commission do not indicate the nature of the businesses. The documents do, however, note that the joint shareholder in the businesses with Mr Andrews is former staffer and fellow traveller on the former premier's secretive China trip, one 'Marty' Zheng Mei.[280]

For all the controversy about his China policies, my search of the Victorian Parliament's Hansard records reveals that he had no reason to mention that country in the 2021, 2022 and 2023 sitting years. Andrews' strategy was driven entirely by himself along with a tiny number of personal staff and an even smaller number of senior public servants. Andrews had little or no concern for public accountability and even less interest in any federal attempts to constrain his actions. Andrews' China Dream combined a seemingly perfect mix of domestic ethnic political campaigning and the opportunity to access PRC investment and trade dollars.

Starting at a time when all political parties in all Australian jurisdictions were chasing PRC money, Andrews remained on the China bandwagon long after the federal government realised that the real China story was about managing risk, not just gorging on opportunity. By that stage Andrews was too invested. He did not pause to consider the risk. He may have thought that intelligence and strategic worries were overstated and, in any event, not within his remit. Advising his South Australian Labor counterpart Peter Malinauskas on the art of government, Andrews said: "Find your three crisis issues and make it all about that. Don't admit where you got it wrong and do the *mea culpa* thing. It feels good today but they will just beat you over the head with it."[281] I doubt that Andrews ever realised that he was really being cultivated through the whole process by a political machine far more sophisticated than even the Victorian Labor party. The Chinese Communist Party played Andrews for a fool and briefly won their political prize: Victoria's endorsement of Xi's Belt and Road plan.

Postscript: Prosperity by any means

Daniel Andrews was prominently back in the Australian media when he attended a remarkable show of Chinese military strength in Beijing at the "Victory over Japan" military parade held on the 3 September 2025. Andrews was photographed in a remarkable lineup of some of the world's least attractive authoritarian leaders including Vladimir Putin President of Russia, Kim Jong Un the North Korean leader, Alexander Lukashenko the President of Belarus and Masoud Pezeshkian the President of Iran.[62]

The most significant photograph of Andrews was him shaking hands with President Xi Jinping of China. It was reported in Australia that this image would be worth substantial money to Andrews in showing his closeness to the senior Chinese leadership. Andrews was by no means the only former democratic leader to attend. Bob Carr, former foreign minister and premier of NSW, attended but he had the good sense to avoid watching the military parade from the Tiananmen Square podium. Remarkably, two former New Zealand Prime Ministers attended: Helen Clark and John Key, all of course invited by China as a way of trying to demonstrate international support for Xi Jinping.

The *Australian Financial Review* observed that Andrews was likely to attract Chinese business interests because of his close political connections in Australia and evident approval by the senior Communist Party leadership in Beijing. An anonymous Chinese business source was quoted by the *Australian Financial Review* as saying, "It could be proof he [Andrews] has real access. I couldn't get a meeting with your Prime Minister but if I paid this guy maybe I could."[63]

As a private citizen Andrews can of course pursue whatever business interests he likes. It seems clear that his main commodity is not personal charm but rather using his contacts in Australia and China. Convenient to the perception of Andrews' access in Australia, the *Herald Sun* reported on the 11 June 2025 that he and Prime Minister Anthony Albanese had lunched at the Melbourne restaurant, Gimlet. The story was accompanied by multiple photos of the Prime Minister and Andrews drinking wine together.[64] Readers should understand that Prime Ministers have the wherewithal to hold meetings away from the camera. If photographs are taken it's because the people being photographed want this information to become public.

Andrews continues to pursue his Chinese business interests with his colleague Marty Mei, with whom he has formed a number of companies, including Forty Eight and Partners, created in January 2024, along with new advisory businesses Wedgetail Partners and Glencairn Street. In Chinese numerology the number 48 is an auspicious number meaning "prosperity by any means".[65]

The *Australian Financial Review* reported that it had spoken to three investors doing business in China and Australia who had been approached by Mai in the last 12 months. They described "Mai's pitch as somewhere between 'an all-access pass to the wealthiest people in China' and 'maybe they would [the Chinese] fill out a little boring forms in Australia.'" None of those who received the pitch said they would engage Andrews' services, but they agreed that the Andrews handshake with Xi would be "worth a fortune" in winning clients in China.[66]

On 14 September 2025 Premier Jacinta Allan issued a statement entitled "Victoria is an old friend of China" a day before leaving for Beijing with a Labor parliamentary delegation. She claimed that she would be "developing Victoria's new China strategy and taking it with me overseas". *The Australian* reported that the strategy will be released in China.[67] Why was there no consultation or discussion about this policy in Victoria? Was the federal government consulted on such a sensitive foreign policy issue?

Allan's statement said: "in an era of divisive Trump-style rhetoric here and abroad, I want to make the case that Victorians from overseas are a proud part of our story to the world."[68] Kowtowing to China and insulting the Americans in one brief media statement shows that Victoria's Labor leadership still aspires to run a foreign policy separate from Canberra. Premier Allan is locked on the same course as her predecessor, without regard to the Chinese Communist Party's aggressive militarism, so amply on display at the parade viewed by Daniel Andrews.

9

Why this is a necessary book

Scott Hargreaves

It is said that 'history is written by the victors', and Daniel Andrews and the political machine he built and bequeathed to his successors definitely occupy the commanding heights of institutional power in Victoria. Opportunities to contest the decisions and the vandalism of institutions undertaken by Andrews when in office were few and dealt with harshly; through rhetorical and actual persecution. In the hollowed out civic culture and increasingly squeezed non-government sector in the state of Victoria, the exit of Andrews from formal political roles is no guarantee that any balanced accounts will emerge organically. Indeed, his continuing influence within the ALP at state and federal levels will further reduce the incentive for such bravery.

Truly, this situation is the opposite of what Marc Antony said of Caesar, when he said of reputations that:

> The evil that men do lives after them;
>
> The good is oft interred with their bones.

In this case, there are precious few independent institutions with the vitality and resources to challenge the more hagiographic accounts of Andrews' achievements. The 'good' will be recycled and retailed in the lead up to the 2026 state election, while the various evils will be buried – interred – or justified as the necessary means to shared ends.

In this chapter I venture three propositions: that there is more to political leadership than victory; that the health of our democracy and culture requires more than the mandate of the majority; and that there is a difference between pursuing victories within the forms of liberal democracy and the Westminster system, and dismantling those norms and destroying that system in order to permanently neuter or destroy real or perceived enemies.

Sceptics may say, 'well he wouldn't be the first political leader in Australia to seek to do so', but that would be to miss that point that he was the first to *succeed.*

One of the default assumptions of most academics and the left – but I repeat myself – is that authoritarianism and 'strong leadership' is generally a feature of 'the right' of the political spectrum.[282] Therefore learned studies would inevitably be commissioned into state premiers such as Sir Joh Bjelke-Petersen (Queensland), Sir Henry Bolte (Victoria), and Sir Thomas Playford (South Australia). Indeed, my very first published article was a review of a compilation of essays decrying the impact of the Kennett government in Victoria, which was very much in that vein.[283] It focused on the then-bogeyman of 'economic rationalism'.

To labour the point: many of the issues regarding governance identified in this chapter are not unique to the Andrews government, but my assertion is that they will be underreported and/or – in the perceived interests of balance – be wrapped into generic analyses of issues that are allegedly of equal concern across all Australian governments. Judgements which differentiate between degrees of harm can and should be formed. It should also be noted that I for one would be happy to draw a contrast with the Bracks and Brumby ALP governments, which also achieved electoral success, but which did not leave in their wake the ruined landscape of hollowed-out institutions for which Andrews bears particular responsibility.

Certainly the scope for applying the lens to Andrews is wide open.

When he announced his retirement as premier, political editor of the *Australian Financial Review*, Phillip Coorey, astutely observed:

> Andrews was a cult figure in Australian politics, built on a ruthless leadership style, which included crushing dissent and discrediting critics while buttressed by the unshakeable loyalty of his followers. If not quite Trumpism, then like Sir Joh; the more he was criticised, the more popular he became.
>
> Even his resignation, which came without notice and gave the party just a day to replace him, was designed to lock in his preferred candidate and socialist left factional colleague, Jacinta Allan, by not giving others time to mobilise. Control to the last.
>
> More than any other in recent years, his was a one-man government, empowered by a shrewd media strategy that largely rejected traditional outlets and spoke directly to his supporters via social media.
>
> The rise of the #istandwithdan social media movement during the pandemic acted as a praetorian guard. Progressive voters allegedly capable of critical thought, instead swore blind allegiance to a politician, abusing and attacking anyone in the media and elsewhere who dared criticise or question Andrews' handling of the pandemic.

To be sure, some working journalists have done their part. Chip Le Grand wrote a not uncritical account of the lockdowns, and Tim Colebatch noted that Sumeyya Ilanbey in her biography[284]:

> Pulls no punches. Daniel Andrews emerges from the book as a highly successful, hard-working, utterly determined, socially progressive despot – with little respect for people who get in his way or for the democratic infrastructure in which he has to operate.[285]

But where are the deeper meta-accounts of the institutional bastardry of the Andrews government, from people who are meant to take an interest in such matters? A search through Google Scholar and academic databases reveals few if any such critical publications.

The conservative journal *Quadrant* definitely had its critiques,[286] as did – at the other end of the spectrum – *Green Left,* which challenged Andrews' claim to be 'the most progressive state'.[287]

But in the peer-reviewed literature we could only find one peer-reviewed study which grappled with the *style* of the Andrews government, in the manner of Costar and Economou's study of Kennett (which had been produced while he was still in office). That is, apart from studies which focused on specific issues like Covid management or the (mis)management of the Commonwealth Games. In that one study, Swinburne University academic David Hayward, set out to establish that "the Andrews government did not actually break with the recent neoliberal past". Neoliberalism for Professor Hayward is a disparaging term, and embodies a critique from the left echoing the 20th century language bemoaning economic rationalism.

And so, this book has been published by the IPA to fill a gap, and to establish that such a critique of both performance and style can and should be mounted. It covers only some of the most important aspects of public administration, and my purpose in this chapter is to suggest potential lines of further inquiry arising from broader considerations of the institutional frameworks within which we conduct ourselves in a liberal democracy.

The tyranny of the majority

One of the great frustrations of attempting to discuss the legacy of the Andrews government is that his electoral success is seen to inherently legitimise whatever measures he took. 'Winners are grinners' is the maxim, and much reference is made to his dominance of opinion polls and actual elections. Moreover, the perceived hopelessness of the state opposition is reason enough to excuse all measures. To be fair, this is a fault of the binary system of politics. The same could be said of the facile nature of most coverage of American politics, in which one's views are reduced to being 'pro' or 'anti' Trump.

The proper context is an understanding of democratic politics that stretches back as far as Aristotle, and was well expressed by Alexis de Tocqueville in his masterly study:

> Tocqueville coined the phrase and was greatly concerned with the risk of Government becoming a "*tyranny of the majority*", when the rights or interests of the minority can be, quite legally and democratically, trampled by the majority. Democracies are more prone to this than even monarchies precisely because the cloak of popular sovereignty legitimises the centralisation of power.

In Australia, the risks are amplified since, as Sir Keith Hancock famously put it in 1930, "Australian democracy has come to look upon the state as a vast public utility, whose duty it is to provide the greatest happiness for the greatest number".[288] Andrews' political success came as he was seen as 'the tireless, manic *doer*; the man that *gets things done*'.[289]

The risks are more pronounced at the state level than they are in Canberra. The Australian Constitution provides the overarching law that governs all governments, but in addition provides very specifically for a separation of powers. In 1915 Sir Isaac Isaacs in a notable High Court judgement said:

> ... (in the Constitution) we find delimited with scrupulous care, the great branches of Government. To use the words of Marshall C.J. in Wayman v. Southard: "the difference between the departments undoubtedly is that the legislature makes, the executive executes and the judiciary construes the law.[290]

By contrast, the Constitution of Victoria is a regular Act of Parliament, the malleability of which was indeed emphasised by Andrews through frequent symbolic changes such as the absurd provisions concerning the State Electricity Commission of Victoria (see also Kevin You's chapter in this volume). Further, the legislature's role in governance was cast aside to an unprecedented role, as outlined in the chapters by Begg and Bagaric in this volume.

The ethical collapse of the Victorian government

In September 2020 I appeared on an IPA Podcast, *Looking Forward*, attempting to come to grips not just with the impact of lockdowns, not just on my out-of-control beard, but on the entire governance framework then in place in Victoria. I said:

> The institutions that have served us so well, one by one have been cast aside: Parliament's been cast aside, Cabinet Government's being cast aside, free speech has been cast aside (and also) civil liberties. All the institutions that were patiently built up over centuries have just been thrown away. And it's…not only is that galling in its own right – I mean, we should maintain all of those institutions, even if they were the most inefficient and stupid way to manage on the earth because they have legitimacy as elements of liberal democracy – but we've cast all them aside.
>
> And what we actually have is not better decision making – it's dysfunctional decision making. This is exactly what we saw in Soviet Russia and China. The more you centralise power, the harder it is for actual information about what's actually going on to reach the top.[291]

To take these and related points in turn:

- At the time the government had suspended sittings of Victoria's Legislative Assembly, and when the Legislative Council continued to sit in defiance of the Premier's will, his ministers refused to cooperate or answer questions.[292]
- Mere administrative regulations (rather than legislation) were being used to enact unprecedented restrictions on daily life.
- The Victorian ALP was at that time run by two administrators appointed by the National Executive, and all state committees were suspended.[293]
- The Westminster traditions of cabinet government – by which the executive arm is accountable through ministers to parliament – had been substituted for one in which

each department secretary was "directly accountable to the Premier".[294]

- The Victorian ALP, which had seen a period of intense but somewhat balanced competition between Andrews' Socialist Left faction and the 'ALP Right' faction, was being transformed into one where dominance of the former was such that after the 2022 election fully seven MPs (including two ministers) shifted from the Right to the Socialist Left in order to maintain their standing.[295] (The role of Jacinta Allan, Andrews' then Deputy, now Premier, in bartering favours for the CFMEU in return for political support, was later the subject of a detailed report in the *Australian Financial Review*,[296] one which provides additional context to the chapter on industrial relations and construction blowouts by John Lloyd.)
- Regarding free speech, not only were protest activities made illegal by administrative *fiat*, but Zoe Buhler – as described by Morgan Begg in his chapter – was arrested without warrant in her own kitchen for the 'crime' of publicising a potential protest.
- Andrews had intimidated and then suborned the media through the device of daily press conferences at which only members of the supine Parliamentary Press Gallery were made welcome, and which were livestreamed.

Clearly something more was going on than a government temporarily accreting power to itself to deal with a temporary emergency. This was one man accreting power to himself, heedless of the damage to countervailing institutions of governance, following a pattern that pre-dated the arrival of the Covid-19 virus and was continued until the day he left office (when his control extended to ensuring his hand-picked successor was installed).

In 2021, two journalists from *The Age* concluded:

> Charges of politicising the public service are not new. Nor are they

> confined to Victoria. In Canberra, the Prime Minister appointed his chief of staff to head the public service. And since the Whitlam government there has been a uniquely Australian tradition of career public servants also spending some time working for a minister as part of their private staff.
>
> The current situation in Victoria is something different. Over the past several months *The Age* has examined how power is wielded in this state. For anyone who values Westminster notions of how government decisions should be made, the findings are confronting.[297]

In searching for theories and precedents to understand what was going on, I asserted then (and stand by now) that a single best fit of available options was achieved by the model of "Ethical Collapse" originally outlined by Marianne M. Jennings in her 2006 book, which had first been drawn to my attention when working for a listed company as an adviser on sustainability.[298] Drawing on examples like that of Enron, Jennings identified seven signs that ethical collapse is imminent:

- Pressure to maintain numbers;
- Fear and silence;
- Young 'uns around a bigger-than-life CEO;
- A weak board;
- Conflicts of interest;
- Innovation like no other; and
- Goodness in some areas atoning for evil in others.

In Victoria there is evidence of deep concerns relating to all seven of these dimensions.[299]

The numbers the premier recounted in his daily interminable press conferences are those of 'cases' and deaths. His key aim was for zero cases over a 14-day period in November (2020), something not achieved anywhere in the world.

"Fear and silence" was maintained by ruthless overlordship of his own party, policing of social media by an army of DanBots (so-called, though not automated but definitely anonymous and hence better referred to as sockpuppets[300]) and the organised #IStandWithDan campaign, and a complicit media which has benefited from the propaganda campaign by dint of being (for the first time in decades) a prime conduit of information to the public (the premier addressed a captive Parliamentary Press Gallery in a windowless room for 120 days in a row, working very hard to not substantively answer any undesired questions). The opposition was silenced by not having access to the public and televised forum of parliament – particularly the lower house (closed for 'health reasons').

The pandemic just exacerbated Andrews' tendency to centralise power into his own hands, bypassing the norms of cabinet government and destroying accountability. He relied on (apparently) more than 100 of his own staff, whom we can presume to have been mostly 'young' and suitably subservient.

While the impacts of punitive lockdowns are felt almost entirely in the private sector, the premier's electoral power base is in the public sector and those reliant upon it. In the June quarter of 2020, wages paid to private workers in Victoria fell by $1.91 billion, while those paid to the public sector increased by $88 million. If you want evidence of a conflict of interest, it is that a 2 per cent pay rise for public servants went ahead as scheduled, in the middle of what was then the biggest recession we've ever had. As one of my IPA colleagues has said, decision-makers "have not incurred any of the costs of their reckless lockdown measures, yet they decide when and how the private sector workforce can go back to work".[301]

There was great pressure to innovate as Victoria followed the lead of so many countries by attempting – for the first time in human history – to defeat a virus through lockdowns. The only precedent was that established by the Peoples Republic of China. Failures in hotel quarantine and contact tracing indicated the state's capacity did not keep pace with the leader's desire to innovate.

Finally, there is the moral dimension: "goodness in some areas atoning for evil in others". Clearly the Premier was convinced that all measures taken (and maybe some more under consideration) could be justified for the good of preventing the deaths otherwise recounted in his grim daily toll (see point 1, above). The most charitable explanation I have read is that he was personally devastated by the deaths of the aged in nursing homes – the tally of which he read out daily – and he was determined that it end.

This, however, blinded him to the moral and ethical problems with the measures he ordered, and even to *other* deaths that will pile up but which are counted in ledgers outside his narrow system (suicides, poverty-related conditions, deferment of health-care etc). Needless to say, speculation about comorbidities and related issues regarding the deceased were *verboten.*

Lest anyone believe the last sentence above is merely my own rhetorical flourish, I refer you to *Australian Financial Review* economics editor, John Kehoe, writing at about this time:

> Victorian Premier Daniel Andrews claims the "science" leaves him with "no choice" but to continue indefinite lockdowns …
>
> Alarmingly, anyone who challenges the government overreach is shouted down for ignoring his increasingly self-selective and short-sighted "data" and "science".
>
> It's reminiscent of America's Vietnam War disaster – historian Max Hastings recounts that the US kept doubling down on its misguided strategy because president Lyndon Johnson blocked a "full and open debate" about the evolving facts.[302]

It took a brave intervention by Sky News host and News Ltd columnist Peta Credlin to break the spell of Andrews' hermetically sealed media briefings and get to the heart of the inconsistencies in the governments' defence of the hotel quarantine debacle.[303]

The disintegrating bulwarks of democratic governance

For a long time the progressive left in Australian was acutely aware of the temptation of 'authoritarian' governments (perhaps because in the 50s and 60s these were mostly of the right), and thus sought to create or bolter institutions which could keep it in check. The ALP can claim much of the credit for the spread of Freedom of Information laws, the establishment of the office of Ombudsman (and the later expansion of its powers), and an enhanced role for the Auditor-General.

In respect of the important role of Ombudsman, the pattern was set from the start:

> When Deborah Glass became Victoria's first female ombudsman 10 years ago, there was no press release issued by the state government.
>
> "I was offended, it was complete radio silence," she said.
>
> "And this was from a government that put out a press statement to announce the opening of an envelope."[304]

The issues were serious:

> "Politicisation can take many forms. It is not just the hiring of people with political affiliations. It is also the closing down or marginalisation of apolitical, independent voices."
>
> "Creeping politicisation is a reality in Victoria, and requires urgent attention," Victorian Ombudsman Deborah Glass said.[305]

And so, neither did it end well:

> "One of the things I found most disappointing is the lack of respect to the findings of integrity agencies and attempts to dismiss that," she said.
>
> "We saw this last year with the previous Premier's attempts to label a report as educational, [which found the Andrews government improperly awarded a multi-million-dollar health contract] in fact it was exposing some pretty serious misconduct.

"I think that's a bad look for government."[306]

In a similar vein we have the reflections of former Supreme Court judge Robert Redlich, who had been commissioned to investigate the use of public funds and staff resources for state ALP branch stacking. He later identified the risks of 'grey corruption' in a speech to the University of Melbourne:

> In Victoria, we can see this concentration [of resources into Daniel Andrews' office] occurring with the number of staff in the Premiers Private Office (PPO), increasing from around 20 in 2011 to 87 in 2019-20 and at the time of this paper in excess of 90.
>
> [The Andrews government] has centralised governance even more than during Jeff Kennett's premiership more than 20 years ago, when staff jokingly referred to ministers as 'warm props' to the dominant Premier.[307]

Spring Street's sad simulacrum of Westminster traditions

It may be easy, but it would also be facile to say that the dominance of Daniel Andrews and his allies only occurred because of the weakness or ineptness of the state opposition.

Facile because such a criticism would not address any of the concerns expressed in this chapter. Defeating one's political opponents through the electoral system is, after all, the essential task of all political parties. The question here is whether that drive for power has extended beyond the electoral process to encompass all perceived barriers to the execution of the singular vision of one man. To 'blame' the loser of a street fight who has fallen to the ground for then allowing themselves to also be kicked in the head is to misunderstand the nature of the context.

It also needs to be noted that Daniel Andrews was determined to change the electoral laws, and did so, in ways that have done long term damage to the opposition's ability to hold the government to account and to present as an alternative government.

This view reflects the IPA's long-standing critique that various electoral 'reforms' around Australia which prohibit donations are wrong in principle. (The issues of principle were well articulated in the 2010 US Supreme Court decision, *Citizens United.*[308]) Emerging evidence would also suggest they have the effect of uniquely harming the non-labor side of politics.

In 2018 we explained that amendments to Victorian electoral law then afoot would undermine freedom of speech and limit democratic participation, by introducing:

> an effective cap of $4,000 per four-year election cycle, beyond which it would be unlawful for an individual to make a political donation, an extremely unusual limitation, in effect placing a restriction on donors, not recipients.
>
> A cap on individual donors would be a significant hindrance on freedom of speech and political communication, because freedom of speech is more than a protection on merely literally speaking about public policy issues. Thousands of Australians exercise their freedom of speech indirectly, by supporting political parties and candidates whose values and policies they support.[309]

Criticism of the laws came not only from the IPA, though others perhaps focused less on the overall principle at stake than the disproportionate impact on smaller parties and independents (and the Teals, a party in drag) attempting to gain a foothold in the Victorian parliament. As reported by the ABC:

> Lawyer Kiera Peacock said the Victorian laws unfairly limited the freedom of political communication without a legitimate reason, such as public safety …
>
> Centre for Public Integrity executive director Catherine Williams said the rules were grossly unfair and a serious deficiency of the state's donation laws.
>
> "It's highly problematic that only the legacy parties are able to benefit from them, and independent candidates don't even have the ability to set one up," Ms Williams said.[310]

In May 2023 an Electoral Review expert panel was appointed by the state to review the operation of the *Electoral Legislation Amendment Act 2018*. The 2018 amendment introduced a broad electoral finance regulation regime, including disclosure requirements, funding, reporting, and enforcement provisions. The panel was tasked with examining whether the *Electoral Act 2002* should be further amended to provide a cap on political expenditure and whether such a cap should apply generally or to specific persons, as well as various other matters. The expert panel's report was completed in November 2023 and tabled in the state parliament on 5 March 2024. The IPA released an analysis of this report in December 2024, finding that

If the recommendations are accepted, they threaten to have a chilling effect on civil society and political participation by constraining freedom of political discourse. Specifically, the analysis finds:

- The recommendation to broaden the definition of 'political expenditure' is arbitrary and would constrain political discourse by restricting the ability of people to participate in issue-based advocacy about policy matters they care about.
- Putting more individuals and entities on a public register will deter involvement in election-adjacent activities, stifling democratic participation.
- The unfettered allowance of in-kind support as well as illusory restrictions on affiliation fees typically enjoyed by the political left will create an uneven playing field that the panel purports to level.
- The proposal to abolish the rights of 'nominated entities' to transfer funds to nominating political parties is not justified by the expert panel and would entrench a structural bias in favour of major parties on the political left.[311]

Conclusions

The bulk of this volume concerning the legacy of Daniel Andrews is concerned with the measurable negative impacts of his administration, including a dramatic escalation in the cost of government, spiralling public debt, and lingering harms from lockdowns almost without parallel from any jurisdiction in the world.

It would be a shame, though, if the reader merely concluded that these represent mere failings in public administration, or ascribe them to more or less typical pattern of a government rewarding its natural constituencies to the exclusion of others, less favoured.

This chapter has been more concerned with more qualitative evaluations. It examined the impact on the political culture of Victoria occasioned by a premier who may not be singular amongst politicians in believing that it is right that the 'winner takes all', but who is perhaps unique in combining this view with almost unmatched capabilities and ruthlessness in pursuit of political goals.

As others have observed, Andrews entire career has been in political management, and he's clearly very good at it.

His style, to reproduce the quote referenced by Peter Jennings in his chapter, is perhaps uniquely founded on fomenting division:

> Find your three crisis issues and make it all about that. Don't admit where you got it wrong and do the *mea culpa* thing. It feels good today but they will just beat you over the head with it.[312]

Adam Creighton in his chapter says that it might take a decade or more to tackle the impact of the waste and financial mismanagement of the Andrews/Allan governments. How much longer will it take to restore the health of Victoria's liberal democracy and vitality to the independent institutions essential to its functioning? It is to be hoped that arising from the publication of this volume civic-minded public intellectuals, researchers, and elected representatives, will take seriously the task of identifying the damage and the solutions.

Afterwords

Ross Du Vernet (Group Chief Executive Officer, Dexus)

"The lack of leadership and direction there means that it's going to be tough for the foreseeable future."

Australian Financial Review, 28 February 2025

Shayne Elliott (former Chief Executive Officer, ANZ Bank)

'[Victoria is] one of the toughest places [to do business]. Look at the payroll tax, why are we taxing something that's good…we are taxing employers for giving people jobs…'

3AW Melbourne, 11 July 2023

Kevin Gallagher (Chief Executive Officer and Managing Director, Santos)

"If I think about Queensland, South Australia, Western Australia — these are very supportive, very development friendly jurisdictions. Victoria? North Korea."

Herald Sun, 28 May 2025

David Marriner (founder, Marriner Group)

"Areas are tired and run down ... Elizabeth Street at Flinders Street was supposed to be a glamour mall. Now it is just filthy, there is no way you can feel safe there."

The Age, 12 September 2025

Brian McNamee (Chairman, CSL)

"Without doubt, it's very obvious that we've been not well governed for a long time from a financial perspective, that is clear, the government spending has been too high, and many projects have been poorly evaluated and shouldn't have been done; and clearly the No. 1 skill would appear to be recruiting more people to work in the bureaucracy."

Australian Financial Review, 2 October 2024

"I was in Sydney last week meeting many very senior fund managers and the lunch thematic was Victoria is uninvestable … the pain will last a decade or more given the fiscal mismanagement of the last 10 years, it's reckless,"

Australian Financial Review, 25 November 2024

Meg O'Neill (Chief Executive Officer and Managing Director, Woodside Petroleum)

"It is really puzzling, though, that the state that was built on the back of oil and gas is now at a stage where due to political reasons … ideology has stood in the way of sensible energy policy here in Victoria."

Melbourne Mining Club, 6 February 2025

Nigel Satterley (Founder and Chief Executive, Satterley Property Group)

"It's like Victoria has got a financial haze over it. Tobin Brothers have more activity in their North Melbourne mortuary than downtown Melbourne. It's dead."

Herald Sun, 13 September 2024

Rob Scott (Chief Executive Officer and Managing Director, Wesfarmers)

"The only area where we're seeing stronger growth in Victoria is the sale of home security products within Bunnings."

Australian Financial Review, 28 August 2025

Ryan Stokes (Chief Executive Officer and Managing Director, Seven Group Holdings)

"I'd say development capital is probably fleeing Victoria for other jurisdictions where there aren't the same land tax penalties, where there isn't the same windfall gain tax, etcetera."

Australian Financial Review, 11 February 2025

Endnotes

Introduction

1. Rachel Baxendale and Samantha Hutchinson, "Daniel Andrews declares Victoria 'the most progressive state' after election landslide" (*The Australian*, 24 November 2018).

2 See Phillip Coorey, "Without trust, our institutions lose authority. Just ask Trump" (*The Australian Financial Review*, 31 October 2024).

3 Sumeyya Ilanbey, *Daniel Andrews: The Revealing Biography of Australia's Most Powerful Premier* (Allen & Unwin, 2022) 20.

4 Ibid.

5 Ibid 135.

6 Rachel Baxendale, "Daniel Andrews puts IBAC through spin cycle" (*The Australian*, 19 April 2023).

7 Rachel Baxendale, "Ombudsman Deborah Glass hits back at Daniel Andrews over IBAC report" (*The Australian*, 26 April 2023).

8 Rachel Baxendale, "Victorian Ombudsman Deborah Glass finds 'creeping politicisation' in public service" (*The Australian*, 6 December 2023).

9 Terry Barnes, "The Victorian Coalition 1999-2023: A Permanent Opposition?" in Scott Prasser and David Clune (eds), *The Art of Opposition* (Connor Court Publishing, 2024) 355.

1 Point of no return?

The chronic mismanagement of Victoria's finances

10 Anthony Walker, *Australia State Ratings at Risk as Fiscal Discipline Wanes* (S&P Global Ratings Australia, February 2025).

11 Ibid.

12 Department of Treasury and Finance (Vic), "Coronavirus (COVID-19) reporting" (Online, updated 14 October 2024). An alternative estimate from the Institute of Public Affairs put the total Victorian Covid spending at $79.4 billion: Morgan Begg and Daniel Wild, *Hard Lessons: Reckoning the economic, social, and humanitarian costs of zero-covid* (Institute of Public Affairs Research Report, September 2022).

13 Rohan Smith, "Victoria Premier's China trip an exercise in distancing herself from Daniel Andrews" (*News.com.au*, 17 September 2025).

14 James Murphy, "The Making & Unmaking of East-West Link" (Doctoral thesis, Swinburne University of Technology, 2019).

15 IFM Investors, "Australian superannuation funds announce $15 billion Melbourne Airport 'Super Train'" (Media release, 16 September 2018).

16 David Crowe and Angus Thompson, "Australians pay the price for CFMEU tactics, figures show" (*Sydney Morning Herald*, 20 July 2024).

17 Richard Willingham, 'Labor walks a tightrope to clean up the CFMEU while keeping the powerful union onside' (ABC News, online, 20 July 2024).

18 Lachlan Clark, *Australia's Public Sector Surge* (Institute of Public Affairs Research Report, December 2024).

2 Liberties lost:

The assault on Victoria's freedoms

19 Morgan Begg, *States of Emergency: An Analysis of Covid-19 Petty Restrictions* (Institute of Public Affairs Research Report, April 2020).

20 Ben Edwards et al., 'Variation in policy response to COVID-19 across Australian states and territories' (Blavatnik School of Government Working Paper 2022/046, June 2022).

21 Judd Boaz, 'Melbourne passes Buenos Aires' world record for time spent in COVID-19 lockdown' (*ABC News*, online, 3 October 2021).

22 *Public Health and Wellbeing Act 2008* (Vic) s 200(1).

23 Morgan Begg, 'An analysis of Victoria's public health emergency laws (1865-2020)' in Augusto Zimmermann (ed), *Fundamental Rights in the Age of Covid-19* (Connor Court Publishing, 2020) 57-74.

24 Morgan Begg, 'Vaccine mandates on Victorian parliamentarians unconstitutional: IPA' (Institute of Public Affairs Media Release, 19 October 2021).

25 Daniel Andrews, 'Safe access zones to protect women's right to medical privacy and dignity' (Media release, 27 November 2015).

26 Australian Associated Press, 'Laws banning protests near abortion clinics faces constitutional challenge', *The Guardian* (3 August 2017).

27 Daniel Andrews, "Well, the bad news is that the Liberals are still on the warpath about Safe Schools, a brilliantly effective program designed to stamp out bullying, not pile it on," (Media release, 16 March 2016).

28 Australian Associated Press, "Daniel Andrews says he won't take advice 'from bigots' on Safe Schools", *The Guardian* (15 May 2016).

29 Daniel Andrews, X (25 July 2016): https://twitter.com/DanielAndrewsMP/status/757341930816622593?lang=en.

30 Daniel Andrews, X (22 January 2021): https://twitter.com/DanielAndrewsMP/status/1352425597687930881.

31 Patrick Durkin, "Andrew Thorburn cancelled as Essendon CEO after 24 hours", *Australian Financial Review* (4 October 2022).

32 Patrick Durkin, "Thorburn warns workers face being cancelled over religion", *Australian Financial Review* (5 October 2022).

33 Essendon Football Club, 'Statement on behalf of Dave Barham' (4 October 2022).

34 Daniel Andrews, X, 7 April 2020. https://twitter.com/DanielAndrewsMP/status/1247351432241508352.

35 Morgan Begg, 'Andrews vs the Christians", *The Spectator Australia* (February 2021).

36 Greg Sheridan, "Victorian election: Daniel Andrew's crusade against Christianity", *The Australian* (25 November 2022).

37 *Change or Suppression (Conversion) Practices Prohibition Act 2021* (Vic) s 5.

38 Daniel Andrews, Facebook, 10 December 2020. https://mk-mk.facebook.com/100044472997869/videos/718296382133990.

39 *Equal Opportunity (Religious Exceptions) Amendment Act 2021* (Vic).

40 Department of Justice and Community Safety, 'Victorian government response into anti-vilification protections' (Online, 2 September 2021).

41 Department of Health, *Australian Health Management Plan for Pandemic Influenza* (August 2019).

42 *R v Dudley & Stevens* (1884) 14 QBD 287.

43 Morgan Begg, *Daniel Andrews' Pandemic Bill: The Attack on Our Democracy* (Institute of Public Affairs Research Report, November 2021).

44 Morgan Begg, *Powers of Detention in Victorian Pandemic Legislation* (Institute of Public Affairs Research Report, March 2022).

3 Trashing the rule of law - with impunity: The erosion of criminal justice in Victoria

45 *Criminal Organisations Control Amendment (Unlawful Associations) Act 2015* (Vic).

46 *Domestic Animals Amendment (Puppy Farms and Pet Shops) Act 2017* (Vic).

47 Premier of Victoria, 'New Outdoor Smoking Bans to Protect Victorian Diners' (29 July 2017) <https://www.premier.vic.gov.au/site-4/new-outdoor-smoking-bans-protect-victorian-diners>.

48 Premier of Victoria, 'Victoria to Have Nation's Strictest Donation Laws' (18 September 2017) <https://www.premier.vic.gov.au/victoria-have-nations-strictest-donation-laws>.

49 *Electoral Legislation Amendment Act 2018* (Vic) ss 48(1), 58; *Electoral Act 2002* (Vic) ss 206, 217D.

50 *Electoral Legislation Amendment Act 2018* (Vic) s 44; *Electoral Act 2002* (Vic) 218(5A).

51 On 3 October 2021, Melbourne had spent a total of 245 days in pandemic lockdown, surpassing the 234-day lockdown in Buenos Aires: Judd Boaz, 'Melbourne passes Buenos Aires' world record for time spent in COVID-19 lockdown', *ABC News* (Online, 3 October 2021).

52 For an overview of the nature of the restrictions that were imposed, see Morgan Begg, *States of Emergency: An Analysis of Covid-19 Petty Restrictions* (Institute of Public Affairs Research Report, April 2020).

53 *Charter of Human Rights and Responsibilities Act 2006* (Vic) s 12.

54 Ibid s 15.

55 Ibid s 17.

56 Joseph Lelliott, Andreas Schloenhardt and Ruby Ioannou, 'Pandemics, Punishment, and Public Health: COVID-19 and Criminal Law in Australia' (2021) 44(1) *UNSW Law Journal* 167, 169.

57 Mirko Bagaric, 'The Civil-isation of the Criminal Law' (2001) 25(4) *Criminal Law Journal* 197.

58 Caitlin Cassidy, 'Victoria Covid update: police arrest 44 people and fire rubber pellets during Melbourne construction protests', *The Guardian* (online, 21 September 2021).

59 See, eg, Victoria, 'Care Facilities Directions (No. 50)', *Victoria Government Gazette*, No S 643, 19 November 2021, 105.

60 See Shannon Deery, 'How many Covid fines have really been paid', *Herald Sun* (online, 9 November 2021).

61 Premier of Victoria, 'State of Emergency Declared in Victoria over COVID-19' (16 March 2020) <https://www.premier.vic.gov.au/state-emergency-declared-victoria-over-covid-19>. Under the *Restricted Activity Directions (Restricted Areas) (No 20)* s 22, issued pursuant to the *Public Health and Wellbeing Act 2008* (Vic) s 200, 120 penalty units awaited those disobeying the *Directions*.

62 (1989) 167 CLR 348 [7]. See also *Veen v R (No 2)* (1988) 164 CLR 465, 472.

63 Lucy Beers, 'Coronavirus: Police fine kids at Melbourne skate park and tennis players in Maribyrnong', *7 News* (online, 15 April 2020).

64 *Crimes Act 1958* (Vic) ss 22–23.

65 Lelliott, Schloenhardt and Ioannou (2021) 196.

66 For example, Melbourne went into its sixth lockdown with less than 12 hours' notice: 'Victoria enters sixth lockdown in response to new mystery COVID-19 cases', *ABC News* (5 August 2021).

67 For example, the *Restricted Activity Directions (Victoria) (No. 23)* for lockdown six in Melbourne were published after midnight 6 August 2021, the day they commenced.

68 'Victorian Premier Daniel Andrews fined for COVID rule breaches after being filmed without a mask', *ABC News* (online, 8 October 2021).

69 Fines Victoria, *Report to Attorney-General under section 53D of the Infringements Act 2006 - Victoria Police processes for the internal review of COVID-19 fines* (n.d.) 4.

70 *R v Dudley & Stephens* (1884) 14 QBD 273; [1881–85] All ER Rep 61, 67.

71 Lord Devlin, *The Enforcement of Morals* (Oxford University Press, 1965).

72 Lelliott, Schloenhardt and Ioannou (2021) 168.

73 Tom R Tyler, *Why People Obey the Law* (Yale University Press, 1990).

74 Australian Associated Press, 'Inquiry reveals 50,000 Covid-related fines issued in Victoria', *The Guardian* (online, 18 May 2022).

75 Ibid.

76 Callum Godde, 'Barely one in 10 Victorian COVID-19 fines paid in full', *Canberra Times* (online, June 9, 2023).

77 Ibid.

78 Ibid.

79 Ibid.

80 See Lelliott, Schloenhardt and Ioannou (2021) 169.

81 Roy Morgan, *As Victorians' ratings for Police fall, two themes emerge: The 'Lawyer X' scandal and COVID enforcement* (Article No 8523, 29 September 2020).

82 Ibid.

83 The other matter that contributed to the decline was the 'Lawyer X' scandal, in which police used a lawyer as an informer in criminal cases.

84 Brianna McKee, 'Senior Victoria police officer Krystle Mitchell resigns, claims most cops "don't believe" in COVID rules', *Sky News* (online, 9 October 2022).

85 Ibid.

86 See, eg, 'People protesting against coronavirus lockdown arrested in Melbourne amid clashes with police', *ABC News* (online, 13 September 2020).

87 See *Charter of Human Rights and Responsibilities Act 2006* (Vic).

88 See Shannon Deery, 'The massive number of Covid fines still outstanding as Victorians refuse to pay', *Herald Sun* (online, 21 November 2023).

4 All eggs in one basket: The deliberate undermining of Victoria's energy security

89 Department of Energy, Environment and Climate Action (Vic), *Victoria's 2035 Emissions Reduction Target*, (May 2023).

90 Josh Gordon, 'Victoria's power dilemma: Reliability, resilience and a 40-year-old plant', *The Age* (online, 15 February 2024).

91 Australian Energy Market Operator, *2023 Electricity Statement of Opportunities* (August 2023).

92 Kevin You, *The Denmark Fallacy and South Australia's Rocky Renewable Energy Transition* (Institute of Public Affairs Working Paper 01/25, April 2025).

93 Interview with Chris Bowen (Sarah Ferguson, Television Interview, 31 August 2023).

94 Kevin You, "Net Zero Pulling the Plug on Australian Manufacturing" (Institute of Public Affairs, media release, 6 June 2022).

95 Ben Potter, Macdonald-Smith and Simon Evans, 'Alcoa smelter ordered to power down as AEMO takes action amid Victoria, SA heat', *Australian Financial Review* (online, 25 Jan 2019).

96 Australian Energy Regulator, *Quarterly volume weighted average spot prices – regions* (online, 2025).

97 Scott Hargreaves, Daniel Wild and Kevin You, *Liddell The Line In The Sand* (Institute of Public Affairs Research Report, 30 May 2023).

98 Scott Hargreaves, "Unrealistic Unreliable Unaffordable" (2022) 74(2) *IPA Review* 16.

99 Energy Australia, "Yallourn Power Station" (online, 2020).

100 AGL, "How we source energy', (online, 2023).

101 Daniel Wild, "AGL's Loy Yang Closure to Leave Families in the Dark and Electricity Bills Up 21%" (Institute of Public Affairs, 30 September 2022).

102 Loy Yang B, "Sustainability Report FY22", Latrobe Valley Power (online, 11 November 2022).

103 Perry Williams, "Alinta faces more pressure over Loy Yang B coal power plant", *The Australian* (online, 20 October 2022).

104 Scott Hargreaves, *The Australian Achievement and its Opponents: Selected Essays* (Connor Court Publishing, 2024) 92.

105 Kevin You and Daniel Wild, *Australia's Net Zero Energy Crisis: An analysis of the electricity price implications of net zero emissions by 2050* (Institute of Public Affairs research report, June 2022).

106 Kevin You, *NSW Government must intervene now to save Eraring and stop power price increases* (Institute of Public Affairs Parliamentary Research Brief, August 2023).

107 Ben Potter, Angela Macdonald-Smith and Simon Evans, "Alcoa Smelter Ordered to power down as AEMO takes action amid Victoria, SA heat", *Australian Financial Review* (online, 25 Jan 2019); Australian Energy Regulator, "AER reports on high wholesale electricity prices in Victoria and South Australia om 24 and 25 January 2019" (online, 26 March 2019).

108 Angela Macdonald-Smith, "Fresh coal power outage hits as NEM resumes", *Australian Financial Review* (online, 24 June 2022); Australian Energy Regulator, "Wholesale markets quarterly – Q2 2022", (online, 6 September 2022).

109 Alan Moran, "The grim cost of firming up solar and wind", *The Spectator* (online, 20 March 2024).

110 Daniel Wild, *The Economic and Employment Consequences of Net Zero Emissions by 2050 in Australia* (Institute of Public Affairs Research Report, April 2022).

111 Saxon Davidson, "AEMO Highlights Need to Keep Reliable and Affordable Baseload Generation on the Grid" (Institute of Public Affairs, media release, 31 August 2023).

112 Australian Energy Management Operator, "2023 IASR Assumptions Workbook", *2024 Integrated System Plan (ISP): 2023 - 24 inputs, assumptions and scenarios*, (online, 8 September 2023)

113 James Lofting and Shae Kirby, "Amendment to the Victorian Planning Provisions Pushes Victoria Towards an Environmentally Friendly Future", *HWL Ebsworth Lawyers* (online, 8 August 2022).

114 Jacinta Allan and Lily D'Ambrosio, "Gas Roadmap Drives Down Energy Bills and Emissions", *Premier of Victoria* (online, 1 July 2022).

115 Broede Carmody, Mike Foley and Lachlan Abbott, "Goodbye, gas stoves: Victoria to ban gas from new homes by 2024", *The Age* (online, 28 July 2023).

116 Saxon Davidson, "Voters Must Say No to Labor's Naïve Plan to Make Victoria Nearly Totally Reliant on Green Energy by 2035", *Sky News Australia* (online, 21 November 2022).

117 Alan Finkel, "Say no to nuclear, and yes to gas-fired power", *Australian Financial Review* (online, 2 August 2023).

118 Mark Ludlow, "States hit for 'demonising' gas", *Australian Financial Review* (online, 28 February 2023).

119 Kevin You and Morgan Begg, *Wire Consequences: Analysis of the cost and impact of nationwide electrification* (Institute of Public Affairs Working Paper 03/24, September 2024).

120 Tony Wood and Guy Dundas, "Flame Out: The future of natural gas", *Grattan Institute* (online, November 2020).

121 Tristan Edis, "The two facts to consider before writing off Dictator Dan's gas ban," *Australian Financial Review* (online, 2 August 2023).

122 Kevin You and Morgan Begg, *Wire Consequences: Analysis of the cost and impact of nationwide electrification* (Institute of Public Affairs Working Paper 03/24, September 2024).

123 Tony Wood, Alison Reeve, and Esther Suckling, "Getting off gas", *Grattan Institute* (online, June 2023).

124 Gavin Maguire, "Clean energy investing loses lustre despite climate crisis", *Reuters* (online, 20 September 2023; Johnathan Leake, "Electricity prices 'must rise by 70pc to pay for more wind farms'", *The Telegraph*, (online, 25 October 2023).

125 Alan Moran, "The grim cost of firming up solar and wind", *The Spectator* (online, 20 March 2024).

126 Kieran Rooney, "Victorian offshore wind farms may supply power to grid by 2025", *The Herald Sun* (online, 11 March 2023).

127 Scott Hargreaves, "New SEC a Dependable Source of Cheap Politics", *Herald Sun* (online, 17 March 2023).

128 Tim Callanan, "Premier Jacinta Allan outlines Victoria's plan to revive the State Electricity Commission", *ABC* (online, 26 October 2023).

129 Royce Millar and Josh Gordon, "Victoria's new-look SEC could sell power direct to homes and businesses", *The Age* (online, 4 February 2023).

130 Patrick Durkin, "'Profound slowdown': Alan Finkel quits Victoria's SEC", *Australian Financial Review* (online, 23 June 2023).

131 Australian Energy Market Operator, *2023 Electricity Statement of Opportunities* (August 2023).

132 Gus McCubbing and Patrick Durkin, "Andrews' $1b SEC 'stunt' left in budget dark", *Australian Financial Review* (online, 26 May 2023).

133 Scott Hargreaves, "New SEC a Dependable Source of Cheap Politics", *Herald Sun* (online, 17 March 2023).

134 Gus McCubbing and Patrick Durkin, "Andrews' $1b SEC 'stunt' left in budget dark", *Australian Financial Review* (online, 26 May 2023).

135 Net Zero Australia, "How to make net zero happen" (online, July 2023).

136 Jacinta Allan, "The SEC Is Back: Accelerating Victoria's Renewable Future" (online, 26 October 2023).

5 Dumbing down:
Social engineering in the Victorian education system

137 Alex White, 'Taxpayers to be slugged $45,000 to change slogan on Victorian numberplates', *Herald Sun* (14 February 2015).

138 Aisha Dow and Mark Hawthorne, 'Victorian election 2014: Daniel Andrews to change number plates to the Education State if Labor wins', *The Age* (5 November 2014).

139 Victorian Curriculum and Assessment Authority, "VCE Unit Completion Outcomes – 2022" (accessed online, 28 August 2024).

140 Adam Carey, "Making it Sexy: Teachers hope revamp will save VCE Australian history," *The Age* (28 June 2021).

141 Victorian Curriculum and Assessment Authority, *Victorian Certificate of Education: History Study Design* (Available online, 2020) 54-64.

142 State Library Victoria, 'Power and resistance (1788-1913)', *VCE Australian history – units 3 & 4* (Research Guide, updated 19 July 2024) <https://guides.slv.vic.gov.au/vceaushist/power>.

143 Victorian Curriculum and Assessment Authority, 'VCE History Study Design 2022–2026' 54.

144 State Library Victoria, 'From custodianship to the Anthropocene (1950-2010)', *VCE Australian history – units 3 & 4* (Research Guide, updated 19 July 2024).

145 Victorian Curriculum and Assessment Authority, 'VCE History Study Design 2022–2026' 56.

146 Larissa McLean Davies et al., "Changing the Subject: Text selection and curriculum development in VCE English 1990" in Tim Dolin, Jo Jones, and Patrcia Dowsett (eds), *Required Reading: Literature in Australian Schools Since 1945* (Monash University Publishing, 2017) 175.

147 Lana Starkey, *Illusion of Choice: New rules mandate woke texts in Victorian schools* (Institute of Public Affairs Research Note, February 2024).

148 For details of these examples see Matthew French, 'Respecting difference: An analysis of the Australian Safe Schools program and parental rights in education' (2018) 9 *The Western Australian Jurist* 102, 116,121.

149 Premier of Victoria, 'Well, the bad news is that the Liberals are still on the warpath about Safe Schools, a brilliantly effective program designed to stamp out bullying, not pile it on.' (Online statement, 16 March 2016).

150 Kevin Donnelly, "Safe Schools Coalition not so safe," *The Catholic Weekly* (30 September 2016).

151 Ibid.

152 Henriette Cook, 'Confusion reigns in Andrews government over Safe Schools program', *The Age* (7 March 2016).

153 Amelia Walters, "Bestiality references allegedly made during presentation at Renmark High School," *ABC News* (4 April 2024).

154 North Western Melbourne Primary Health Network (NWMPN), "Doctors in schools program improving care experiences for patients, providers" (online, accessed 28 August 2024).

155 Government of Victoria, "Doctors in secondary schools" (online, accessed 28 August 2024).

156 Fiona Russell et al., *COVID-19 in Victorian ECEC and Schools: An analysis of COVID-19 in ECEC and schools and evidence-based recommendations for opening ECEC and schools & keeping them open* (Murdoch Children's Research Institute, November 2020).

157 Ibid 13, 64.

158 See Julie Sonnemann and Peter Goss, *COVID catch-up: Helping disadvantaged students close the equity gap* (Grattan Institute, June 2020).

159 Peter Butterworth et al., "Effect of lockdown on mental health in Australia: evidence from a natural experiment analysing longitudinal probability sample survey" (2022) Vol. 7 No. 5 *Lancet Public Health* e427.

160 Anthea Rhodes et al., *Mental health of children and parents in Victoria during the covid-19 pandemic* (Royal Children's Hospital Melbourne, May 2022).

161 VicHealth, *VicHealth coronavirus Victorian wellbeing impact study* (October 2021) 4.

162 VicHealth, *Coping with Coronavirus: Second interim report* (February 2021) 4-6.

163 Catherine Underwood, Lisa De Bortoli, Sue Thomson, *PISA 2022: Reporting Australia's results, Volume 1 Student performance and equity in education* (Australian Council for Educational Research, 2023).

164 Catherine Underwood, Lisa De Bortoli, Sue Thomson, *PISA 2015: Reporting Australia's results* (Australian Council for Educational Research, 2015); Catherine Underwood, Lisa De Bortoli, Sue Thomson, Marina Schmid *PISA 2018: Reporting Australia's results Volume 1 Student Performance* (Australian Council for Educational Research, 2018).

165 Kylie Hillman et al, *Australia's results from PIRLS 2021: Progress in International Reading Literacy Study* (The Australian Council for Educational Research, 2023).

166 Meredith Peace, "Why the Liberals don't deserve your vote" (AEU Media release, online, 7 November 2022).

167 Sydney Criminal Lawyers, "Dan's Dictatorship: Victorian Premier may have lied about curfew advice" (online, 12 September 2020); Melissa Cunningham, "Doctors stoush over Victoria's extended lockdown," *The Sydney Morning Herald* (online, 10 October 2020).

168 Tom McIlroy. "Victoria teacher shortage: Andrews government unveils $229m scheme to pay for degrees", *The Guardian* (Online, 12 September 2023).

6 Unions empowered: Cost blowouts and delays in Victoria's public service and major projects

169 See Adam Creighton's chapter earlier in this book; see also Daniel Wild and Kevin You, *Victoria on the Edge: Debt, Deficits, and Unsustainable Growth* (Institute of Public Affairs Research Report, October 2022).

170 Victorian Auditor-General's Office, *Major Projects Performance Reporting 2023* (Independent Assurance Report to Parliament 2023-24: 9, November 2023).

171 Parliamentary Budget Office, *Suburban Rail Loop: Cost to Build and Operate East and North Sections* (2024).

172 Victorian Auditor-General's Office, *Major Projects Performance Reporting 2023* (Independent Assurance Report to Parliament 2023-24, 9 November 2023). See also Department of Treasury and Finance (Vic), *Victorian Budget 2024-25, Budget Paper No.2 – Strategy and Outlook* (2024) 53.

173 Holly McKay, 'Victoria State Election 2014: Labor pledges to recruit 450 extra firefighters', *Herald Sun* (18 November 2014).

174 See Electoral Matters Committee, *Inquiry into the Conduct of the 2014 Victorian state election* (May 2016) 143. See also UFU Victorian Branch, Submission No. 39 to Joint Standing Committee on Electoral Matters *Inquiry into campaigning at polling places* (20 July 2015).

175 Paul Sakkal and Sumeyya Ilanbey, "Victorian MP calls out trolling as government refuses to release sexism report", *Sydney Morning Herald* (online, 19 May 2021).

176 AAP, "Vic firefighters, minister in ugly row", *9News* (online, 11 December 2015); Sakkal and Ilanbey (2021).

177 'Statement from the minister for emergency services' (29 March 2023).

178 Fire and Rescue Victoria, *Annual Report 2021-22* (2022) 10, 121.

179 Department of Treasury and Finance (Vic), *Victorian Budget 2023-24 Paper No.5 – Doing What Matters* (2023) 18.

180 Fire and Rescue Victoria, *Annual Report 2021-22* (2022) 110.

181 Shannon Deery and Mitch Clarke, "Ten thousand volunteer firefighters flee since Daniel Andrews came to office", *Herald Sun* (online, 6 March 2023).

182 Shannon Deery, "IBAC probe into Victorian Government dealings with United Firefighters Union delayed", *Herald Sun* (online, 19 March 2023).

183 Judy Skatssoon, "Hotel quarantine procurement processes found lacking," *Government News* (online, 9 July 2021).

184 Transcript of Proceedings, Inquiry into the Covid-19 Hotel Quarantine Program (Melbourne, Day 23, 23 September 2020) 1937.

185 Independent Broad-based Anti-corruption Commission, *Operation Daintree Special Report* (April 2023).

186 Department of Environment, Water, Land and Planning, *Annual Report 2021-22* (2022) 107, 113.

7 Failure on every front: The economic legacy of Victoria's Covid-era decisions

187 See for instance Andrew Hedgman, "'Never necessary': Former chief health officer Brett Sutton admits some Covid-19 measures were mistakes", *news.com.au* (online, 23 September 2025).

188 Gigi Foster and Paul Frijters, *Hiding the Elephant: The Tragedy of COVID Policy and its Economic Apologists* (Institute of Labor Economics Discussion Paper Series, No. 15294, May 2022).

189 See for examples, Martin Lally, "A cost–benefit analysis of COVID-19 lockdowns in Australia" (2022) 40 *Monash Bioethics Review* 62–93; Morgan Begg and Daniel Wild, *Hard Lessons: Reckoning the Economic, Social, and Humanitarian Costs of Zero-Covid* (Institute of Public Affairs Research Report, September 2022); Gigi Foster and Sanjeev Sabhlok, *Do Lockdowns and Border Closures Serve the "Greater Good"? A cost-benefit analysis of Australia's reaction to COVID-19* (Connor Court Publishing, 2022).

190 Department of Treasury and Finance (Victoria), *Victorian Budget 2023/24: Doing What Matters: COVID Debt Repayment Plan* (May 2023) 1.

191 Australian Associated Press, 'FACT CHECK: Did the government's COVID-19 policies really save 40,000 Australian lives?', *SBS Online* (20 April 2022).

192 Australian Bureau of Statistics, *COVID-19 Mortality in Australia: Deaths registered until 31 March 2022* (20 April 2022).

193 Australian Bureau of Statistics (2020–2022), *Life Expectancy, 2020-2022* (8 November 2023).

194 Government of Victoria, *Key Statistics* (Webpage, published May 2022 and updated 14 July 2023).

195 Births Deaths and Marriages Victoria, *Death Statistics* (Webpage, n.d.).

196 Department of Health, *COVID-19 Pandemic Plan for the Victorian Health Sector* (10 March 2020): Unavailable on the department website, archived at <https://web.archive.org/web/20231210012127/https://sanjeev.sabhlokcity.com/Misc/Victoria%20-COVID-19-pandemic-plan.pdf >.

197 Premier of Victoria, *Commonwealth Games Costs Too High at Over $6 Billion* (Media Release, 18 July 2023).

198 Jeffrey Wilson, 'Deep dive: Australia's missing migrants and the labour market', *Ai Group* (Online, 6 October 2022).

199 Tom Burton, 'Australia's wealth gap on the rise with inequality worst since 1950', *Australian Financial Review* (30 April 2023).

200 Gigi Foster and Sanjeev Sabhlok, *Do Lockdowns and Border Closures Serve the "Greater Good"? A cost-benefit analysis of Australia's reaction to COVID-19* (Connor Court Publishing, 2022).

201 Paul Frijters et al, 'A Happy Choice: Wellbeing as the Goal of Government' (2020) 4(2) *Behavioural Public Policy* 126–165.

202 State of Life, 'A new gold standard for measurement and evaluation, plus praise for the new WELLBY measure' (Online article, 4 August 2021); New Zealand Treasury, *The Treasury's CBAx Tool* (Last updated 21 December 2023).

203 Paul Frijters and Christian Krekel, 'Wellbeing cost-effectiveness analysis and existing approaches' in *A Handbook for Wellbeing Policy-Making: History, Theory, Measurement, Implementation, and Examples* (Oxford; online edn, Oxford Academic, 2021).

204 Office for National Statistics UK, *Personal well-being in the UK: April 2022 to March 2023* (7 November 2023).

205 A transcript of my testimony was published by the Victorian parliament: Public Accounts and Estimates Committee, *Inquiry into the Victorian Government's Response to the COVID-19 Pandemic* (Transcript, 12 August 2020). The shell of the CBA is available on Victoria's Public Accounts and Estimates Committee's website.

206 Paul Frijters, Gigi Foster and Michael Baker, *The Great Covid Panic: What happened, why, and what to do next* (Brownstone Institute, 2021) 89.

207 Gigi Foster, "Early estimates of the impact of COVID-19 disruptions on jobs, wages, and lifetime earnings of schoolchildren in Australia" (2020) 23(2) *Australian Journal of Labour Economics* 129, 135.

208 See Edelman, *Trust Barometer 2023* (2023).

209 Rebekah Barnett, 'Australian medical regulator finally relaxes Covid gag order', *Brownstone Institute* (26 December 2023).

210 Cameron Murray and Paul Frijters, *Rigged: How networks of powerful mates rip off everyday Australians* (Allen and Unwin, 2022).

211 Meg Mundell, *Weathering the Storm: How the Victorian Building and Construction Industry Survived Covid-19* (Research Report prepared for Incolink by Hatch Insight, December 2023) 2.

212 See for example Spencer Kimball, 'The Covid pandemic drives Pfizer's 2022 revenue to a record $100 billion', *CNBC* (31 January 2023); Leroy Leo and Patrick Wingrove, 'Moderna sees up to $4 billion in 2023 sales from private market for COVID shots', *Reuters* (4 August 2023).

213 Brownstone Institute, 'Had you known, would you have taken the jab?' (5 December 2023).

214 E.g., Pierre Kory, 'New FOIA'ed data reveal NY vaccine clinics called ambulances to be "on standby"', *Brownstone Institute* (29 December 2023).

215 Gigi Foster et al., "Into the abyss: how bad can the covid vaccine story get?", *Brownstone Institute* (online, 31 July 2025).

216 E.g., see press release issued on 1 October 2021, entitled 'Vaccination Required to Protect Workers and Victoria'.

217 Zoe Zaczek, 'Daniel Andrews says watching the sunset is "not in the spirit" of Melbourne's COVID-19 lockdown', *Sky News Australia* (20 August 2021).

218 Greg Jericho, 'Ditch the rose-coloured glasses: Australia's GDP is going backwards', *The Guardian* (7 December 2023).

219 Chloe Whelan, 'Thousands more Aussies dying as "excess deaths" rise', *news.com.au* (7 April 2023).

8 The China dream: Victoria's unprecedented foreign policy activities

220 The core of Xi Jinping's ideology is the delivery of the "China dream", set out in 2017 as "building China into a 'great modern socialist country that is rich, strong, democratic, cultured, harmonious, and beautiful' by 2050." Chinese policy objectives shape around delivering that ambition. Internationally, Xi sees the delivery of China's dream requires the weakening of the United States and its allies, discouraging these countries from countering China and, "exacerbating internal divisions within countries, especially democracies". Steve Tsang and Olivia Cheung, *The Political Thought of Xi Jinping* (Oxford University Press, 2024) 28, 183.

221 'Tony Abbott declares Australia "open for business"', *SBS News* (online, 8 September 2013).

222 Commonwealth, *Parliamentary Debates*, House of Representatives, 17 November 2014, 12724 (Xi Jinping, President of the People's Republic of China).

223 Commonwealth, *Parliamentary Debates*, House of Representatives, 17 November 2014, 12718 (Tony Abbott, Prime Minister).

224 Commonwealth, *Parliamentary Debates*, House of Representatives, 17 November 2014, 12721 (Xi Jinping, President of the People's Republic of China).

225 Curiously the *Partnerships for Prosperity* strategy is no longer available on the Premier of Victoria's website. Click one of the many internet links to the document and you will be taken to a web page titled "Oops! …Sorry, we couldn't find the page you were looking for." The strategy is available here: https://minefreeglenaladale.org/wp-content/uploads/2021/04/Victorias-China-Strategy.pdf.

226 Jeremy Page, Carol E Lee and Gordon Lubold, 'China's President Pledges No Militarization in Disputed Islands: Statement at White House offers

few details, leaving some questioning commitment', *Wall Street Journal* (online, 25 September 2015).

227 State of Victoria, *Victoria's new China Strategy: Partnerships for prosperity* (2016) 14.

228 For an outstanding assessment of relations between Australian states and territories and China, see John Fitzgerald (ed), *Taking the Low Road: China's Influence in Australian States and Territories* (Australian Strategic Policy Institute, 2022).

229 'Chinese company Landbridge to operate Darwin port under $506m 99-year lease deal', *ABC News* (online, 13 October 2015).

230 Helen Davidson, 'Chinese company secures 99-year lease of Darwin port in $506m deal', *The Guardian* (online, 13 October 2015).

231 James Massola, Philip Wen, Brian Robins and Sean Nicholls, 'Treasurer Scott Morrison blocks sale of Ausgrid to foreign bidders', *Sydney Morning Herald* (online, 11 August 2016).

232 Peter Hartcher, *Red Zone: China's Challenge and Australia's Future* (Black Inc., 2021) 53.

233 James Massola, 'Sam Dastyari may have broken federal and NSW Labor Party rules on donations', *Sydney Morning Herald* (online, 7 September 2016).

234 Erin Handley, 'Chinese billionaire blasts 'giant baby' Australia's anti-China agenda in rare interview', *ABC News* (online, 13 February 2020).

235 Chris Uhlmann and Andrew Greene, 'Chinese donors to Australian political parties: who gave how much?', *ABC News* (online, 21 Aug 2016, updated 8 Jun 2017).

236 Christina Zhou, 'China's Belt and Road Forum shows Xi Jinping's "genius marketing ploy" has become "project of the century"', *ABC News* (online, 26 April 2019).

237 Ibid.

238 Ariel Bogle, 'Huawei banned from 5G mobile infrastructure rollout in Australia', *ABC News* (online, 23 August 2018).

239 Christina Zhou, 'China-Australia relations became 'complex' in 2019 with spy claims and human rights abuses', *ABC News* (online, 8 January 2020).

240 Andrews' travel reports are available on the state government website: <https://www.vic.gov.au/dpc-ministerial-travel-reports>.

241 Daniel Andrews, 'Premier's Foreword', *Victoria's New China Strategy: Partnerships for Prosperity* (Victorian Government, April 2016) 3.

242 Sumeyya Ilanbey, *Daniel Andrews: The Revealing Biography of Australia's Most Powerful Premier* (Allen & Unwin, 2022) 33–4, 117.

243 John Fitzgerald, 'Victoria' in John Fitzgerald (ed), *Taking the Low Road: China's Influence in Australian States and Territories* (Australian Strategic Policy Institute, February 2022) 55–6.

244 Ibid.

245 Nia Tam, 'CIC plugs $900m into the Port of Melbourne', *Infrastructure Investor* (online, 2 November 2016) <https://www.infrastructureinvestor.com/cic-plugs-900m-into-port-of-melbourne/>.

246 'DPC travel outcomes report: Daniel Andrews' 2017 travel to China' (Website updated 19 June 2023) <https://www.vic.gov.au/dpc-travel-outcomes-report-daniel-andrews-2017-travel-china>.

247 Department of Foreign Affairs and Trade, *2017 Foreign Policy White Paper* (November 2017) 27.

248 The MoU is no longer available on the Victorian Premier's website, but can be accessed as an excerpt in the following news article: Dan Harrison, 'Victorian Government releases agreement with China on Belt and Road Initiative', *ABC News* (online, 12 November 2018).

249 Premier of Victoria, 'Victoria and China Take Partnership to the Next Level' (23 October 2019) <https://www.premier.vic.gov.au/victoria-and-china-take-partnership-next-level>.

250 Ibid.

251 Premier of Victoria, *Opening Channels For Exchange With Hong Kong* (14 July 2014) <https://www.premier.vic.gov.au/opening-channels-exchange-hong-kong>.

252 Dylan Butts, Molpasorn Shoowong and Meredith Chen, 'Hong Kong's 25 years under China: Protests, politics and tightening laws', *NBC News* (online, 1 July 2022).

253 Premier of Victoria *Opening Channels For Exchange With Hong Kong* (14 July 2014) <https://www.premier.vic.gov.au/opening-channels-exchange-hong-kong>.

254 Anthony Galloway, 'The call never came: Victoria's China deal was done through Premier Daniel Andrews' office', *Sydney Morning Herald* (online, 23 April 2021).

255 Sumeyya Ilanbey, *Daniel Andrews: The Revealing Biography of Australia's Most Powerful Premier* (Allen & Unwin, 2022) 186.

256 Eryk Bagshaw and Anthony Galloway, 'Premier's Belt and Road adviser helped land Labor donation', *The Age* (online, 29 May 2020).

257 Ibid.

258 Steve Tsang and Olivia Cheung, *The Political Thought of Xi Jinping* 148.

259 Richard McGregor, Natasha Kassam and Jennifer Hsu, *Lines blurred: Chinese community organisations in Australia* (Report, Lowy Institute, 2 November 2021) 2.

260 Ibid.

261 Nadia Daly, 'One Belt One Road: NT businesses welcome Chinese investment despite reluctance over "new Silk Road"', *ABC News* (online, 8 August 2017).

262 Rowan Callick, 'One Belt, One Road China advisory group launches in Melbourne', *The Australian* (online, 27 May 2016).

263 Rowan Callick, 'Belt and Road firms need to get engaged, says Aussie expert', *The Australian* (online, 22 May 2017).

264 Australia China Belt & Road Initiative, 'Jean Dong', *Our People* < https://web.archive.org/web/20240311213915/https://acbri.org.au/archived/#jean-dong>.

265 Australia-China Youth Dialogue, *2014 ACYD Delegates* (1 October 2014) <https://www.acyd.org.au/acyd/2014-acyd-delegate-list-released>.

266 Damon Johnston, Remy Varga and Rachel Baxendale, 'Chinese pageant winner Jean Dong's meteoric journey to influence', *The Australian* (online, 28 May 2020).

267 Australia-China Youth Dialogue, *2014 ACYD Delegates* (1 October 2014) <https://www.acyd.org.au/acyd/2014-acyd-delegate-list-released>.

268 Fitzgerald (2022) 56–7.

269 Damon Johnston, Remy Varga and Rachel Baxendale, 'Chinese pageant winner Jean Dong's meteoric journey to influence', *The Australian* (online, 28 May 2020).

270 Jonathan Kearsley, '"There it was, China's list of grievances": How 9News got the dossier at the heart of the latest diplomatic scuffle between Canberra and Beijing', *9News* (online, 23 November 2023).

271 Marise Payne, 'Decisions under Australia's Foreign Arrangements Scheme' (Media Release, 21 April 2021) <https://www.foreignminister.gov.au/minister/marise-payne/media-release/decisions-under-australias-foreign-arrangements-scheme>, citing *Australia's Foreign Relations (State and Territory Arrangements) Act 2020* (Cth).

272 Ibid.

273 Daniel Hurst, 'Federal government tears up Victoria's Belt and Road agreements with China', *The Guardian* (online, 22 April 2021).

274 Premier of Victoria, 'Showcasing Victorian Produce on the Global Stage' (Media Release, 19 October 2021) <https://www.premier.vic.gov.au/showcasing-victorian-produce-global-stage>.

275 Ibid.

276 Will Glasgow, 'Andrews and Morrison part ways again over China trade', *The Australian* (online, 6 November 2021).

277 See ibid.

278 Broede Carmody and Natassia Chrysanthos, 'China-bound Andrews told to stay in his lane amid call for trip transparency', *The Age* (online, 26 March 2023).

279 Sumeyya Ilanbey and Matthew Knott, 'How Daniel Andrews pulled off a China trip shrouded in mystery', *The Age* (online, 1 April 2023).

280 Damon Johnston, 'Director Dan's not just focused on China', *The Weekend Australian* (online, 21 January 2024).

281 Sumeyya Ilanbey, *Daniel Andrews: The Revealing Biography of Australia's Most Powerful Premier* (Allen & Unwin) 294.

9 Why this is a necessary book

282 See for example my old lecturer at Melbourne University, Graham Little, *Strong Leadership: Thatcher, Reagan and an Eminent Person* (Oxford University Press, 1988).

283 Scott Hargreaves, "Kennett's Ferrari" (1999) Vol. 43 No. 10 *Quadrant* 79-81.

284 Sumeyya Ilanbey, *Daniel Andrews: The Revealing Biography of Australia's Most Powerful Premier* (Allen & Unwin, 2022).

285 Tim Colebatch, "What drives Daniel Andrews?", *Inside Story* (online, 24 October 2022).

286 Gavin Silbert, "The Disappearing Rule of Law in Victoria" (2025) Vol. 69 No. 1/2 *Quadrant* 69-72.

287 Arie Huybregts, "How progressive is Victorian labour (sic)?" (2022) *Green Left* Issue 1369.

288 Keith Hancock, *Australia* (Ernest Benn, 1930).

289 James Murphy, "Deciphering the legacy of Danism", *Pursuit* (The University of Melbourne 27 September 2023).

290 *NSW v Commonwealth ('The Wheat Case')* (1915) 20 CLR 54, per Isaacs J.

291 Institute of Public Affairs, *Looking Forward Episode 79: Victorians Have Made Their Bed* (Podcast, September 2020).

292 Kaitlyn Offer and Benita Kolovos, "Vic parliament sitting a bust during COVID", *The Standard* (4 August 2020).

293 Katharine Murphy, "Federal ALP makes extraordinary intervention into Victorian branch-stacking scandal", *The Guardian* (online, 16 June 2020).

294 Chip Le Grand, "As the enemy advances, who's in charge of Victoria's defences?", *The Age* (online, 17 June 2020).

295 Paul Sakkal and Sumeyya Illanbey, "Andrews boosts internal grip on power, two ministers in firing line for demotion", *The Age* (online, 1 December 2022).

296 David Marin-Guzman (2023), "Victorian Premier Jacinta Allan's delicate dance with the CFMEU", *Australian Financial Review* (online, 4 October 2023).

297 Chip Le Grand and Paul Sakkal, "The chosen few: How Victoria is really governed", *The Age* (online, 14 August 2021).

298 Marianne Jennings, *The Seven Signs of Ethical Collapse: How to Spot Moral Meltdowns in Companies... Before It's Too Late* (St Martin's Press, 2006).

299 The following points are reproduced with minimal edits from a contemporaneous article: Scott Hargreaves, "The ethical collapse of Victoria's government", *The Spectator Australia* (online, 12 September 2020).

300 James Purtill, "#IStandWithDan vs #DictatorDan: how fringe accounts gamed Twitter during Melbourne's lockdown", *ABC News* (online, 22 December 2020).

301 Cian Hussey, "Australia Is In A K-Shaped Recession" (Institute of Public Affairs, 8 September 2020).

302 John Kehoe, "Victoria's Daniel Andrews cherry-picks virus 'science'", *Australian Financial Review* (online, 12 October 2020).

303 Ben Graham, "Peta Credlin documentary: Explosive new claim about Victoria's second wave origin", *news.com.au* (online, 1 November 2020).

304 Bridget Rollason, "After a decade in the job, Deborah Glass reflects on her time as Victoria's ombudsman", *ABC News* (online, 5 April 2024).

305 Victorian Ombudsman, "Creeping politicisation of public sector a reality in Victoria: Ombudsman" (media release, online, 6 December 2023).

306 Ibid.

307 Tom Burton, "Why Victoria is vulnerable to grey corruption risk", *Australian Financial Review* (online, 24 November 2022.

308 *Citizens United v FEC*, 558 U.S. 310 (2010).

309 Gideon Rozner, *The Victorian Electoral Legislation Amendment Bill 2018* (Institute of Public Affairs Parliamentary Research Brief, 19 June 2018).

310 Richard Willingham, "Group of independent and minor party candidates to challenge Victoria's political donations laws in High Court", *ABC News* (online, 20 November 2024).

311 Morgan Begg and Mia Schlicht, *No Representation Without Participation: Analysis of proposed changes to Victoria's electoral laws* (Institute of Public Affairs Working Paper 04/2024).

312 Ilanbey (2022) above n 3, 294.

Manufactured by Amazon.com.au
Sydney, New South Wales, Australia

31076645R00105